TEAM JIHAD

How Sharia-Supremacists Collaborate with Leftists to Destroy The United States

By Matthew Vadum

Senior Vice President, Capital Research Center

for the Center for Security Policy

April 2017

For more information about this book, visit SecureFreedom.org

Team Jihad is published in the United States by the Center for Security Policy Press, a division of the Center for Security Policy.

ISBN-13: 978-1545237656
ISBN-10: 1545237654

The Center for Security Policy
Washington, D.C.
Phone: 202-835-9077
Email: info@SecureFreedom.org
For more information, visit SecureFreedom.org

Book design by Bravura Books
Cover design by J.P. Zarruk

Cover photo courtesy of Pamela Hall
TheSilentMajorityNoMore.com

Table of Contents

At a moment when a motley crew of demonstrators, protesters, and violent urban thugs has repeatedly joined forces – not just to make known their unhappiness with the Donald Trump administration, but to bring chaos to American streets and to seek the destruction of our constitutional order – there is an urgent need to understand who is organizing, funding and leading these cabals. Their banners, placards and slogans provide incomplete answers. Indeed, it seems that many of the marchers themselves fail to understand who is pulling the strings that propel the seemingly disparate Muslim Brothers, Black Lives Matter operatives, radical feminists, anarchists and other hard leftists to coordinated confrontation with law enforcement and the rest of American society.

Unfortunately, our preparedness for confronting the array of such forces committed to the destruction of traditional Western values and civilization as enshrined in the U.S. Constitution has faltered badly in the years since the attacks of September 11, 2001. That is due, in no small measure, ironically to the successful influence operations waged against our national security leadership by adherents to the same ideology that animated the attacks of that fateful day: Islam's Sharia doctrine. As a result, that leadership has been rendered incapable of confronting these enemies by name, identifying accurately what impels them, let alone achieving a decisive victory over them and their ideology.

As Matthew Vadum persuasively documents in *Team Jihad: How Sharia-Supremacists Collaborate with Leftists to Destroy the United States*, the jihadists' success in this regard is not entirely attributable to the seductiveness of their information and influence operations. They owe much to the decades-long march of cultural Marxism through the key pillars of American society: academia, faith communities, government (especially national security), law enforcement, and media.

After all, it was communist, leftist, and progressive operatives who successfully promoted the notion that the Judeo-Christian principles laid down by the Founding Fathers were, at best, outmoded and, at worst, a force for ill in the world. In this shared antipathy to the traditional religious values that inspired and nurtured Western civilization, Islam and the left found grounds to make common cause: They could set aside their own divergent ideologies and desired end states for the time being and join forces to bring down America.

The emergence of the contemporary Red-Green axis coincided with – and contributed to – the undoing of a counterintelligence mindset in official U.S. circles. Effectively neutralized was any appreciation of the threat posed

1

by influence operations and, in particular, their perpetrators inside the United States. These dynamics contributed greatly to the collapse of our Intelligence Community's ability to protect against hostile propaganda, whether of the communist or *taqiyya* varieties, and subversive infiltration by their practitioners.

That vulnerability was made all the more ominous by the ties between Western leftists and jihadists who were recruited, trained and, in some cases at least, managed by the Soviet Union and its feared security service, the KGB. Over the years, we have learned much about such operations from declassified information like the Mitrokhin Archive and the Venona Papers. Defectors like Ion Pacepa from Romania's secret police and brilliant researchers like Diana West in *American Betrayal: The Secret Assault on our Nation's Character* have illuminated how communist agents stoked the flames of Islamic terrorism and infiltrated deeply inside the ranks of the U.S. government.

Now, with this newest contribution to the Center for Security Policy's "Civilization Jihad Readers" series, Matt Vadum helps clarify the decades-long collaboration among such forces, collaboration that for too long operated mostly in the shadows. He brings to the work a remarkable record of expertise and scholarship. He is an award-winning investigative journalist, who has published widely on issues related to leftist infiltration and subversion within American society. Mr. Vadum's superbly researched new material and in-depth analysis complements two other books in the series: James Simpson's *The Red-Green Axis: The Left, Islamists and the Erasing of America* and *Star Spangled Sharia: The Rise of America's First Muslim Brotherhood Party,* the first book to document the Muslim Brotherhood's bid to become a political force in the United States.

Highlights of *Team Jihad* include a wealth of historical detail about when and how the left and Islam first made common cause and the myriad ways in which they continue to do so today, notably through the shared use of psychological warfare tools that include name-calling, intimidation, and the distortion and suppression of facts and their opponents' speech. On campus, in the mainstream and social media, and the streets of America, cultural Marxists and jihadis now work hand-in-hand to demean our culture, destroy the nuclear family, trash the nation's heritage and undermine non-Muslim religious communities.

Mr. Vadum also shows how such mutually reinforcing subversion is being underwritten by the left's wealthy donors and foundations. Their shared loathing for America, its traditions and Constitution – and for Western civilization, more generally – has translated into literally billions of dollars expended to weaken Americans' faith in themselves and, thereby, to help undermine the resolve needed to defend constitutional freedoms against both cultural Marxism and Islamic supremacism.

While significant changes in U.S. domestic and foreign policy now are in prospect under the Trump administration, far too much time already has been lost. Most Americans still lack an appreciation of the lead America's enemies have been afforded because of myriad past failures to understand and confront them effectively. They can, nonetheless, see the mayhem exploding all around them, mourn the loss of brave local law enforcement officials and feel outrage at the serial, toxic assaults on their cherished values.

Matthew Vadum has, with his lucid and highly readable style, rendered a real public service by making his extraordinary research accessible to all of us concerned about what is happening to the country we love. While our anti-American foes are clever, hate-filled, tenacious and well-funded, they are now exposed. With their masks pulled off and their nefarious, shared agenda laid bare, they should prove to be no match for an American people informed at last and engaged in the defense of country and Constitution against all enemies, foreign and domestic.

Frank J. Gaffney, Jr.
President and CEO
Center for Security Policy
18 March, 2017

CHAPTER 1

The Left, Dawah and Jihad

"Only a coalition of Marxists and Islamists can destroy the U.S."
— Ilyich Ramirez Sanchez, a.k.a. Carlos the Jackal[1]

The American Left has entered into an alliance of convenience with Islamic terrorists aimed at taking down their mutual enemy: the United States of America. Their psychological warfare is waged against the American people. Their primary tools are name-calling, intimidation, and the suppression of facts. Their wealthy foundations fund nonprofit groups and campaigns focused on transforming our culture to make it Islam-friendly while weakening our resolve to fight Islamic supremacism and the terrorism it deploys against us.

Those who follow the activism of American leftists appreciate their extraordinary, instinctive knack for siding with America's enemies. They live by the ancient aphorism that *the enemy of my enemy is my friend*. They aligned with the monstrous Soviet Union in 1917. Many of them stayed loyal to that foreign power even after mass murderer Josef Stalin's crimes came to light following his death in 1953.

They cheered on Communist Cuba in 1962 when it threatened to inflict mass casualties on the United States using nuclear weapons. To this day, no amount of evidence of the Cuban regime's brutal, exhaustively documented persecution of churchgoers, artists, and homosexuals dissuades them. American radical Medea Benjamin recalled that when she moved to Cuba she felt "like I died and went to heaven."

They supported the totalitarian regime in Communist Vietnam in the 1960s and 70s even while the U.S. waged war against it. Throughout the 1980s, the Left agitated for nuclear disarmament by the United States — but not the Soviet Union. They stood by fanciful, apocalyptic theories like "nuclear winter" which held that nuclear war would lead inevitably to human extinction. After the Islamic terrorist attacks of Sept. 11, 2001, they predictably blamed America for supposedly provoking the Muslim world into murdering Americans.

---

[1] "Europe's Islamist Alliance," by Amir Taheri, *Jerusalem Post*, July 12, 2004, archive.frontpagemag.com/readArticle.aspx?ARTID=12242, May 22, 2016

The very next evening then-obscure community organizer Van Jones, a self-described "communist" and "rowdy black nationalist" who is now a CNN contributor and a fixture of the Democratic Party establishment, participated in a vigil "mourning the victims of U.S. imperialism around the world." In his view the 3,000 people who died during the 9/11 attacks were innocent victims of an unjust system that victimizes everyone. Determined to think the worst about their fellow Americans, Jones, like many commentators on the Left, forecasted a violent racist backlash within the country. "Anti-Arab hostility is already reaching a fever pitch as pundits and common people alike rush to judgment that an Arab group is responsible for this tragedy," he said. The backlash never came.[2]

In the aftermath of the attacks, academics said that America got what it deserved on 9/11. University of Colorado professor Ward Churchill said the financial sector employees killed in the World Trade Center were "little Eichmanns," a reference to Nazi SS officer Adolf Eichmann who helped organize the Holocaust. The victims' deaths were a "penalty befitting their participation in ... the 'mighty engine of profit' to which the military dimension of U.S. policy has always been enslaved."[3] Canadian academic Sunera Thobani attacked the United States saying it "is one of the most dangerous and the most powerful global forces that is unleashing prolific levels of violence all over the world. From Chile to El Salvador, to Nicaragua to Iraq, the path of U.S. foreign policy is soaked in blood."[4]

Although linguist and self-appointed foreign policy expert Noam Chomsky described 9/11 as a "horrendous atrocity," he shrugged that "this is the culture in which we live." He expressed doubt that Osama bin Laden was behind the attacks and said that "the world is ruled by force. The only way we can put a permanent end to terrorism is to stop participating in it," accusing the U.S. of terrorism in Nicaragua, Chile, Costa Rica, Honduras, Argentina, Colombia, Turkey, Vietnam, Laos, and Cambodia. With wry satisfaction he added:

This is the first time the guns have been pointed the other way. For hundreds of years, Europeans have been slaughtering each other and slaughtering people all over the

[2] "Van Jones and his STORMtroopers denounced America the night after 9/11," by Matthew Vadum, *American Spectator*, Aug. 29, 2009, http://spectator.org/19985_van-jones-and-his-stormtroopers-denounced-america-night-after-911/. His group was called Standing Together to Organize a Revolutionary Movement (STORM).

[3] Professor under fire for 9/11 comments," by T.R. Reid, Washington Post, Feb. 5, 2005, http://www.washingtonpost.com/wp-dyn/articles/A76-2005Feb4.html, accessed April 28, 2016

[4] "The speech that shook the country," by Sunera Thobani, Herizons, Winter 2002, http://www.herizons.ca/node/131, accessed April 28, 2016

world. But the Congo didn't attack Belgium. India didn't attack England. Algeria didn't attack France. The world looks very different depending on whether you're holding the lash or being whipped by it.[5]

After 9/11, all of these leftists urged Americans to look inward, to examine the so-called root causes of Islamic hatred of Western Civilization. They said the problem isn't with Islam; the problem is with *us*.

Those on the Left see Muslims as the new underclass. Americans are bullies who have pushed the Islamic world around for far too long. Muslims should not assimilate; Americans should change their culture to accommodate the new arrivals. This is the essence of multiculturalism, that is, the poisonous belief that all cultures are equal, which is the foundation for the claim that America is just another country.

This is also the kind of nihilism in which President Obama believes. "I believe in American exceptionalism, just as I suspect that the Brits believe in British exceptionalism and the Greeks believe in Greek exceptionalism," he said at the outset of his presidency, draining the word *exceptionalism* of meaning.

And no wonder Obama did little more than the bare minimum to defend America from the terrorist onslaught. He rejects (in public, at least) the idea that there is a clash of civilizations under way. To him, Americans and jihadis simply view the world differently. While the president denounced Islamic terrorists publicly – remember he mocked the highly effective savages of Islamic State in 2014 as a "jayvee team" – his actions, such as his support for jihadis in Egypt, Iran, Libya, Syria, and Turkey, told an altogether different story.

Obama is far from alone. Very few on the Left are willing to acknowledge the truth about Islam and its relentless, bloodthirsty drive for expansion and conquest. Obama was blasé about the efforts of jihadis around the world to rebuild the Caliphate, an Islamic state governed by Islamic Law (sharia) that functions as the highest state authority in Islam. The term *caliph* refers to the "Head of the Islamic Community." In early Muslim history the Arabic word meant "literally 'successor' or 'deputy' (i.e. of the Prophet Muhammad)." The title has been claimed by a "variety of dynastic leaders throughout Islamic history[.]" The "technically elective office ... combined *in theory* a spiritual and a secular function, though *in practice*,

---

[5] "Chomsky criticizes US violence," by Sarah H. Wright, Massachusetts Institute of Technology website, Oct. 24, 2001, http://news.mit.edu/2001/chomsky-1024, accessed April 27, 2016

under such dynasties as the Umayyads, it was the latter function which was generally important at the expense of the former."[6]

Both major sects of Islam, Sunni and the much smaller Shia branch, embrace the idea of having Caliphs (or Imams, for the Shi'ites), a ruler over Muslims who seeks to expand the *Ummah*, or the community of Muslims, though they disagree on how such a ruler should be chosen. The last caliphate of note was the Ottoman Caliphate which disintegrated early in the twentieth century. Islamic State, which exercises control over parts of Syria and Iraq and claims to be a sovereign state, was in a hurry, declaring itself a caliphate in 2014. The Muslim Brotherhood also aspires to create a caliphate but wants to do it more gradually using more conventional political methods. Islamic State, which al-Qa'eda sees as moving too far, too fast to impose sharia (the definition of 'extremism' in Islam per Qur'an 2:190), claims to wield authority over all Muslims, though it is unknown how many Muslims actually recognize this claim. In 2014 Islamic State unveiled an ambitious plan to re-conquer for Islam the Iberian Peninsula, the northernmost half of Africa, and large parts of Europe, along with swaths of western Asia including Saudi Arabia and Turkey.[7]

Caliphates don't exactly have admirable human rights records by Western standards. Rather, they rule by Islamic Law, under which inequality between Muslims and non-Muslims, and between men and women, is enforced. Amputation, beheading, concubinage, execution for adultery, apostasy, homosexuality, and slander, flogging, rape and murder of captives, stoning to death, and slavery are all perfectly legal.

The last Caliphate, the Ottoman Empire, was selling non-Muslim girls as sex slaves after the invention of the telephone. A *New York Times* report from 1886 documented the sale of girls as young as twelve, one of them with "light hazel eyes, black eyebrows and long yellow hair." An earlier report from the *London Post* described Turks, "sending their blacks to market, in order to make room for a newly-purchased white girl." This behavior is not a temporary aberration, but dates back to Mohammed's men raping and enslaving non-Muslim women and young girls as a reward for fighting to spread Islam. ... To Muslims, the end of slavery is one of the

---

[6] "Khalifa," *A Popular Dictionary of Islam*, by Ian Richard Netton, NTC Publishing Group, Chicago, 1997, p.143. The italics appear in the original.

[7] "The ISIS map of the world: Militants outline chilling five-year plan for global domination as they declare formation of caliphate - and change their name to the Islamic State," by John Hall, Daily Mail, July 1, 2014, http://www.dailymail.co.uk/news/article-2674736/ISIS-militants-declare-formation-caliphate-Syria-Iraq-demand-Muslims-world-swear-allegiance.html, accessed June 2, 2016

humiliations that they had to endure because of the loss of the Caliphate. Europeans forced an end to the slave trade. The British made the Turks give up their slaves. The United States made the Saudis give up their slaves in the 1960s. (Unofficially they still exist.) When the Muslim Brotherhood took over Egypt, its Islamist constitution dropped a ban on slavery.[8]

Islamic State's atrocities, while horrifying to most people, "are typical of a functioning Caliphate," Daniel Greenfield writes. The "execution of Muslims who do not submit to the Caliph, the ethnic cleansing and sexual slavery of non-Muslims are not aberrations. They are normal behavior for a Caliphate." These acts "that we find so shocking were widely practiced in even the most civilized parts of the Muslim world around the time that the Statue of Liberty was being dedicated in New York City."[9]

The Organization of Islamic Cooperation (OIC), which comprises 56 Muslim countries plus the Palestinian Authority, claims to represent all Muslims everywhere. President Obama apparently agreed with this claim. The OIC "scored a diplomatic coup when the Obama Administration agreed to host a three-day Istanbul Process conference" in Washington, D.C. in December 2011. "In doing so, the United States gave the OIC the political legitimacy it has been seeking to globalize its initiative to ban criticism of Islam."[10]

Scholar Bat Ye'or warns that the OIC is already a "would-be universal caliphate" that wields great power through the European Union, United Nations, and other international organizations. She writes that it has a planning document, "Strategy of Islamic Cultural Action in the West," in which it claims that "Muslim immigrant communities in Europe are part of the Islamic nation." The document also recommends "a series of steps to prevent the integration and assimilation of Muslims into European culture." She adds, "[t]he caliphate is alive and growing within Europe ... It has advanced through the denial of dangers and the obfuscating of history. It has moved forward on gilded carpets in the corridors of dialogue, the network of

---

[8] "It's not ISIS we need to beat – it's the Caliphate," by Daniel Greenfield, FrontPageMag, Dec. 29, 2015, http://www.frontpagemag.com/fpm/261264/its-not-isis-we-need-beat-its-caliphate-daniel-greenfield, accessed June 2, 2016

[9] "It's not ISIS we need to beat – it's the Caliphate," by Daniel Greenfield, FrontPageMag, Dec. 29, 2015, http://www.frontpagemag.com/fpm/261264/its-not-isis-we-need-beat-its-caliphate-daniel-greenfield, accessed June 2, 2016

[10] "'Caliphate Conference' Seeks to Islamize Europe, U.S.," by Soeren Kern, Gatestone Institute website, Feb. 21, 2012, https://www.gatestoneinstitute.org/2866/caliphate-conference, accessed June 2, 2016

the Alliances and partnerships, in the corruption of its leaders, intellectuals and NGOs, particularly at the United Nations."[11]

In 2011, during the Muslim Brotherhood-led uprising in Egypt, Glenn Beck courageously raised the alarm about the reemerging Islamic Caliphate some time before Islamic State formed. Beck warned that the Left was working with jihadis. As Beck's news website recounted, he was mocked and insulted by pundits across the political spectrum for saying that jihadis "in the Middle East are trying to rebuild the caliphate — the government implemented after the death of the prophet Muhammad that derives its authority from and governs by sharia law."[12]

MSNBC's Chris Matthews said the Caliphate idea was "looney tunes" and condemned Beck for "fear mongering," "crazed meanderings," and "Captain Queeg stuff." He added that Beck was a "mad professor." On Matthews's show, Salon's Joan Walsh said Beck "really may be losing his mind" and his statements are "completely crazy."[13]

Left-wing *Time* commentator Joe Klein described Beck as a "free-range lunatic" plagued by "hilarious commie-muslim caliphate delusions." He also labeled Beck a "paranoid-messianic rodeo clown."[14]

The more surprising attacks came from conservatives who apparently had learned nothing from the 1960s, an era of out-in-the-open leftist treachery against the United States. More than a few on the Right suffer from a pathological optimism that prevents them from seeing the true face of the Left. They refuse even to consider the possibility that left-wing Americans are capable of selling out their mother country to Islamic supremacists.

As Beck was sharing his views about the resurgence of Islam, *Commentary*'s Peter Wehner penned a post calling Beck "The Most Disturbing Personality on Cable Television." Relying on the rhetorical equivalent of a "you think you're so smart" schoolyard taunt, he ridiculed

---

[11] "'Caliphate Conference' Seeks to Islamize Europe, U.S.," by Soeren Kern, Gatestone Institute website, Feb. 21, 2012, https://www.gatestoneinstitute.org/2866/caliphate-conference, accessed June 2, 2016

[12] "Glenn Beck Was Relentlessly Mocked for Warning of an Islamic Caliphate. What's He Saying Now That It's Being Seriously Discussed on CNN?" by Erica Ritz, The Blaze, June 16, 2014, http://www.theblaze.com/stories/2014/06/16/glenn-beck-was-relentlessly-mocked-for-warning-of-an-islamic-caliphate-whats-he-saying-now-that-its-being-seriously-discussed-on-cnn/, accessed June 2, 2016

[13] "Matthews Attacks Beck On Caliphate Theory, by Mike Opelka, The Blaze, Feb. 2, 2011, http://www.theblaze.com/stories/2011/02/02/matthews-attacks-beck-on-caliphate-theory/, accessed June 2, 2016

[14] "How Long, Glenn Beck, How Long?" by Joe Klein, Time, Feb. 5, 2011, http://swampland.time.com/2011/02/05/how-long-glenn-beck-how-long/, accessed June 2, 2016

Beck as a self-appointed "solitary Voice of Truth willing to expose the New World Order (complete with references to Van Jones and Code Pink)."[15]

Weekly Standard editor William Kristol laid into Beck with unrestrained glee and *National Review* editor Rich Lowry seconded him.

Beck was suffering from "hysteria," according to Kristol. "When Glenn Beck rants about the caliphate taking over the Middle East from Morocco to the Philippines, and lists (invents?) the connections between caliphate-promoters and the American left, he brings to mind no one so much as Robert Welch and the John Birch Society. He's marginalizing himself, just as his predecessors did back in the early 1960s."[16] Lowry piled on, endorsing what he called Kristol's "well-deserved shot at Glenn Beck's latest wild theorizing."[17]

Yet by 2014, Beck's thinking on Islamic expansionism found support in some quarters of the Obama administration.

Mohamed Elibiary, then a senior adviser to the Department of Homeland Security, said the capture of Iraqi cities by Islamic State was evidence of the "inevitable" return of a Muslim "Caliphate."[18]

Marx and Muhammad

This counterintuitive alliance between leftists and Muslims is nothing new. Islam and the Left overlap. Socialism is commonly believed to have originated in Europe but it also has roots in the Islamic world. The Arabic word for Islamic socialism is *ishtirakiyyah al-Islam*.

Advocates of this Islamic socialist ideology point to the example of Abu Dharr al-Ghifari (unknown - 652 A.D.), a companion of Muhammad who is said to have criticized the accumulation of wealth by the Umayyad Caliphate and urged its coercive redistribution. "When he was speaking of capitalism and the hoarding of wealth and he was strongly defending the wretched, and when he was turning against the aristocrats and the palace-dwellers of

---

[15] "The Most Disturbing Personality on Cable Television," by Peter Wehner, Commentary, Feb. 24, 2011, https://www.commentarymagazine.com/culture-civilization/the-most-disturbing-personality-on-cable-television/, accessed June 2, 2016

[16] "Stand for freedom," by William Kristol, Weekly Standard, Feb. 14, 2011, http://www.weeklystandard.com/stand-freedom/article/541404, accessed June 2, 2016. The word "invents?" appears in parentheses in the original.

[17] "Kristol on Beck," by Rich Lowry, National Review, http://www.nationalreview.com/corner/259072/kristol-beck-rich-lowry, Feb. 5, 2011, accessed June 2, 2016

[18] "Read These Tweets About the 'Inevitable' Return of the 'Caliphate' — the Bigger Story Could Be Who Actually Wrote Them," by Jason Howerton, The Blaze, June 16, 2014, http://www.theblaze.com/stories/2014/06/16/read-these-tweets-about-iraq-takeover-and-return-of-the-caliphate-the-bigger-story-could-be-who-actually-wrote-them/, accessed June 2, 2016

Damascus and Medina, he resembles an extreme socialist like [Pierre-Joseph] Proudhon," according to Ali Shariati.[19]

It is also notable that Muhammad himself created a welfare state in Medina when he ruled it.

In the 1800s Jamal al-Din al-Afghani argued that socialism was an ideology that grew out of Arabian Bedouin traditions before the advent of Islam. Socialism complemented Islam, he believed.

Years before V.I. Lenin, Al-Afghani "proceeded to Islamize the received socialist wisdom." He "preached an Islamic socialism where there would be no class war and where private ownership would be tolerated." He wrote that "socialism is part and parcel of the religion of Islam."[20]

Some of the more famous Islamic socialists in history are Palestine Liberation Organization (PLO) chairman Yasser Arafat, Pakistani Prime Minister Benazir Bhutto, Turkish president Mustafa Kemal Ataturk, Indonesian president Sukarno, and Muammar Qaddafi of Libya. After seizing power, Qaddafi renamed his country the Great Socialist People's Libyan Arab Jamahiriya.

Somali dictator Mohamed Siad Barre claimed that it was easy to fuse Islam and socialism together because each sought to regulate a separate domain.

As far as socialism is concerned, it is not a heavenly message like Islam but a mere system for regulating the relations between man and his utilization of the means of production in this world. If we decide to regulate our national wealth, it is not against the essence of Islam. Allah has created man and has given him the faculty of mind to choose between good and bad, between virtue and vice. We have chosen social justice instead of exploitation of man by man and this is how we can practically help the individual Muslim and direct him to [a] virtuous life.[21]

Although not all Muslims hold left-wing political views, some Muslims and leftists believe they have common interests. As William S. Lind explained, in 1939 two of the bitterest enemies, Nazi Germany and the Union

---

[19] "And once again Abu-Dhar," by Ali Shariati, Iran Chamber Society website, date unknown, http://www.iranchamber.com/personalities/ashariati/works/once_again_abu_dhar1.php, accessed Sept. 20, 2016

[20] Israel and the European Left: between solidarity and delegitimization, by Colin Shindler, Continuum International Publishing Group, London, 2012, p.53

[21] *A Modern History of Somalia*, by Ioan Myrddin, Wilture Enterprises (International) Ltd., 1980, page unknown, as referenced at http://www.africanvault.com/siad-barre-quotes/, accessed May 29, 2016

of Soviet Socialist Republics, found a way to work together for mutual advantage. The two countries formed the mutually advantageous Ribbentrop-Molotov Pact that allowed Adolf Hitler and Josef Stalin to cut Poland in half and start World War II. Of course the non-aggression protocol never saw its second birthday, which ought to be instructive to the leftists aligning with the jihadis who long to slit their progressive throats as soon as they can.

Today Muslim Machiavellis are working with the Left to undermine the United States. Lind says there is a "Marx-Mohammed Pact" in effect.

> **Once again, two sworn enemies, Marxism — specifically the cultural Marxism commonly known as Political Correctness — and Islam, have made a Devil's bargain whereby each assists the other against a common enemy, the remnants of the Christian West.[22]**

The below observations from Lind a decade ago about the process of Islamization in Europe should serve as a warning to Americans as President Donald Trump moves to reform U.S. immigration and refugee resettlement programs that had been importing a steady stream of refugees from Syria and elsewhere who share many of the anti-Western, anti-American, pro-sharia views of the Islamic State they claim to be fleeing. Lind explained:

> **Leftists and Muslims have a mutual short-term interest in keeping the leftist parties in power, and a mutual long-term interest in weakening the traditional culture of Europe. During this third Islamic Jihad, the third Islamic attempt to conquer and subdue the West, leftists all over Europe seem to be opening the gates of Europe from within. "You want to conquer Europe? That's okay. Just vote for us and help us get rid of capitalism and eradicate the Christian heritage of Europe, and we'll let you in. In the meantime, you can enjoy some welfare goodies, and we will ban opposition to this undertaking as racism and hate speech.[23]**

---

[22] "The Marx-Mohammed Pact," by William S. Lind blogging as Fjordman, July 25, 2005, http://fjordman.blogspot.com/2005/07/marx-mohammed-pact_25.html, accessed May 15, 2016.

[23] "Symposium: The Death of Multiculturalism?" by Jamie Glazov, FrontPageMag.com, Sept. 8, 2006, http://archive.frontpagemag.com/readArticle.aspx?ARTID=2695 accessed May 15, 2016. The quotation was offered by Lind during a panel discussion.

CHAPTER 2

An Alliance of Convenience

I t has long been recognized that Islam and the Left can coexist without blowing each other to bits – at least for a while. They can even thrive together because they have much in common.

Months after 9/11 former British Prime Minister Margaret Thatcher compared Islam to communism. "Islamic extremism today, like bolshevism in the past, is an armed doctrine," she wrote. "It is an aggressive ideology promoted by fanatical, well-armed devotees. And, like communism, it requires an all-embracing long-term strategy to defeat it."[24]

Thatcher is far from alone.

Islamic theologian Sayyid Abul A'la Maududi (1903 - 1979), was an intellectual jihadist leader along with his Egyptian contemporary Sayyid Qutb (1903 – 1966), author of *Social Justice in Islam*. Maududi, who founded Jamaat-e-Islami (The Islamic Party) in Pakistan, acknowledged in *The Islamic Law and Constitution* that an Islamic state is necessarily totalitarian.

A state of this sort cannot evidently restrict the scope of its activities. Its approach is universal and all-embracing. Its sphere of activity is coextensive with the whole of human life. It seeks to mould every aspect of life and activity in consonance with its moral norms and programme of social reform. In such a state no one can regard any field of his affairs as personal and private. Considered from this aspect the Islamic state bears a kind of resemblance to the Fascist and Communist states.

Islam has "historic and philosophic ties to Marxism-Leninism," observes Daniel Pipes. Egypt's Qutb "accepted the Marxist notion of stages of history, only adding an Islamic postscript to them; he predicted that an eternal Islamic era would come after the collapse of capitalism and Communism."

Iranian thinker Ali Shariati took works of Frantz Fanon, Che Guevara, and Jean-Paul Sartre and translated them into Persian. Azar Nafisi, author of the 2003 memoir *Reading Lolita in Tehran*, observes that Islam "takes its language, goals, and aspirations as much from the crassest forms of

---

[24] "Islamism is the new bolshevism," by Margaret Thatcher, The Guardian, Feb. 12, 2002, https://www.theguardian.com/world/2002/feb/12/afghanistan.politics, accessed May 1, 2016

Marxism as it does from religion. Its leaders are as influenced by Lenin, Sartre, Stalin, and Fanon as they are by the Prophet."[25]

In *The New Jerusalem*, G.K. Chesterton opined that because both Muslims and communists believe "their simple creed was suited to everybody," they aspire to "impose it on everybody[.]" In the essay "Communism and Islam," Bernard Lewis wrote of the essence of Islam. Although Muslim religious leaders "are very different from the Communist Party[,]" there are "certain uncomfortable resemblances," he argued.

> **Both groups profess a totalitarian doctrine, with complete and final answers to all questions on heaven and earth; the answers are different in every respect, alike only in their finality and completeness, and in the contrast they offer with the eternal questioning of Western man. Both groups offer to their members and followers the agreeable sensation of belonging to a community of believers, who are always right, as against an outer world of unbelievers, who are always wrong. Both offer an exhilarating feeling of mission, of purpose, of being engaged in a collective adventure to accelerate the historically inevitable victory of the true faith over the infidel evil-doers.**

In *The Practice and Theory of Bolshevism*, philosopher Bertrand Russell made the case that Bolshevism and Islam, both of which refuse to tolerate "unbiased examination," reject scientific evidence if it contradicts their worldview. While Christianity and Buddhism "are primarily personal religions, with mystical doctrines and a love of contemplation," Islam and Bolshevism "are practical, social, unspiritual, concerned to win the empire of this world."

Jules Monnerot (1908-1995) in *Sociology and Psychology of Communism* opined that communism was "the Twentieth-century Islam."

> **Communism takes the field both as a *secular religion* and as a *universal State*]; it is therefore ... comparable to Islam ... Soviet Russia ... is not the first empire in which the temporal and public power goes hand in hand with a shadowy power which works outside the imperial frontiers to undermine the social structure of neighboring States. [emphases in original]**

---

[25] "Allied Menace," by Daniel Pipes, National Review, July 14, 2008, http://www.meforum.org/4502/the-islamist-leftist-allied-menace, accessed May 10, 2016

Bernard Lewis also sees similarities between the Muslim and leftist worldviews. Both inspire a deep dogmatic devotion among their adherents.

The traditional Islamic division of the world into the House of Islam and the House of War, two necessarily opposed groups, of which the first has the collective obligation of perpetual struggle against the second, also has obvious parallels in the Communist view of world affairs. There again, the content of belief is utterly different, but the aggressive fanaticism of the believer is the same. The humorist who summed up the Communist creed as "There is no God and Karl Marx is his Prophet" was laying his finger on a real affinity. The call to a Communist Jihad, a Holy War for the faith — a new faith, but against the self-same Western Christian enemy."[26]

Or as Sebastian Gorka put it more simply, "Islam is a totalitarian ideology suffused with religion."[27]

How the Left Makes Excuses for Islam

Left-wingers don't normally come out and explicitly say they hate the United States, its political institutions, and American culture. They tend to do as radical left-wing community organizing guru Saul Alinsky – the *Rules for Radicals* author and inspiration to both Barack Obama and Hillary Clinton – counseled in his 10th rule of "the ethics of means and ends" and "clothe" their arguments "with moral garments." They attack America, emphasizing its shortcomings past and present.

At the same time, they go to great lengths to make excuses for Islam and for Muslim supremacist behavior. They agonize over why so many Muslims hate us. They blame the Christian Crusades that began way back in the 11th century for breeding Muslim animosity toward the Western world. They blame the U.S. alliance with Israel and the presence of American troops in Saudi Arabia for sparking resentment. They blame the U.S. for being too powerful and too wealthy. They blame certain Americans for not showing Islam the respect to which they believe it is entitled.

But leftists sometimes show their hand, speaking with unaccustomed candor about why they sympathize with Islamic supremacism, jihad, and sharia.

---

[26] "5 prominent authors on the parallels between Islam and Communism, by Benjamin Weingarten, The Blaze, Jan. 22, 2015, http://www.theblaze.com/blog/2015/01/22/5-prominent-authors-on-the-parallels-between-islam-and-communism/, accessed May 2, 2016

[27] Sebastian Gorka, on the "John Batchelor Show," June 10, 2016.

Now imprisoned in France, Venezuelan arch-terrorist Ilyich Ramirez Sanchez, a.k.a. Carlos the Jackal, is both a Marxist and a Muslim convert who hates America. "Only a coalition of Marxists and Islamists can destroy the U.S.," he counsels. Bringing down the oppressive, imperialist United States is "the highest goal of humanity."

And only Islam can generate enough "volunteers" for suicide attacks against the United States, Carlos asserts in his book, *Revolutionary Islam* (Editions du Rocher, 2003). He argues for "the destruction of the United States through an orchestrated and persistent campaign of terror." Posing as a humanitarian, he posits that terrorism is "the cleanest and most efficient form of warfare" because the killing of civilians undermines the enemy's morale and ultimately saves the lives of many by bringing the conflict to a swift end.[28]

Carlos claims to have advised Osama bin Laden to forge alliances with "all guerrilla, terrorist, and other revolutionary groups throughout the world, regardless of their religious or ideological beliefs."[29]

Muslims love Carlos right back, according to jihadist journalist Ali Osman Zor. "We believe that bin Laden, like our commander Mirzabeyoglu and our soul-mate Carlos the Jackal, is one of the architects of the new world that will be built following the triumph of Islam."[30]

Al-Qa'eda leader Ayman al-Zawahiri also agrees with Carlos that jihadists should be willing to work with *anybody*. He told followers in 2002 to seek allies among "any movement that opposes America, even atheists.[31]

Jihadists' willingness to work with atheists is striking because atheism is particularly objectionable to Islam. It is punishable by death under sharia and in at least 13 majority-Muslim countries.[32]

Unrepentant Weather Underground terrorist Bill Ayers, a longtime friend of Barack Obama, is a supporter of HAMAS. The self-described small-c

---

[28] Islamic Economics and the Final Jihad, by David Jonsson, Xulon Press, 2006, pp.413, 415

[29] "Europe's Islamist Alliance," by Amir Taheri, Jerusalem Post, July 12, 2004, archive.frontpagemag.com/readArticle.aspx?ARTID=12242, accessed May 22, 2016

[30] "'Kaide' ('Al-Qa'eda') magazine published openly in Turkey," Tempo, Aug. 3, 2005. The article was translated by the Middle East Media Research Institute (MEMRI) and published online on Aug. 7, 2005. See http://www.memri.org/report/en/0/0/0/0/0/0/1432.htm, accessed May 22, 2016

[31] "Europe's Islamist Alliance," by Amir Taheri, Jerusalem Post, July 12, 2004, archive.frontpagemag.com/readArticle.aspx?ARTID=12242, accessed May 22, 2016

[32] "There are 13 countries where atheism is punishable by death," by Abby Ohlheiser, The Wire, Dec. 10, 2013, http://www.thewire.com/global/2013/12/13-countries-where-atheism-punishable-death/355961/, accessed May 22, 2016. According to the article, "The countries that impose these penalties are Afghanistan, Iran, Malaysia, Maldives, Mauritania, Nigeria, Pakistan, Qatar, Saudi Arabia, Somalia, Sudan, United Arab Emirates and Yemen. With the exception of Pakistan, those countries all allow for capital punishment against apostasy, *i.e.*, the renunciation of a particular religion. Pakistan, meanwhile, imposes the death penalty for blasphemy, which can obviously include disbelief in God."

communist also was "involved in provoking chaos on the streets of Egypt in an attempt to enter Gaza with the Free Gaza Movement to join in solidarity with the territory's population and leadership."[33]

Left-wing former lawyer Lynne Stewart adores Islam and its supremacist mission.

Stewart praises Muslim militants as "forces of national liberation." Americans on the left, "as persons who are committed to the liberation of oppressed people, should fasten on the need for self-determination, and allow people ... to do what they need to do to throw off that oppression."[34]

"Islamic revolution is the only hope" for the oppressed peoples of Egypt, Jordan, the Gulf states, and Saudi Arabia, she said in 2002. "If their people see that they want to reinstate a system of law and government that was in existence for hundreds and hundreds of years, I'm not going to judge."

Stewart was convicted in 2005 of providing material support to terrorists. While acting as legal counsel to Omar Abdel-Rahman (a.k.a. the Blind Sheikh) she illegally relayed a message from this man who masterminded the 1993 World Trade Center bombing. The communiqué, from a prisoner who was held incommunicado specifically to prevent him from directing terrorist activities from his prison cell, was "the blessing of a return to violence from a terrorist leader," prosecutor Anthony Barkow said. In it, Abdel-Rahman urged his disciples in Al-Gama'a al-Islamiyya (a.k.a. The Islamic Group), to abandon a ceasefire with the government of Egypt and resume terrorist operations.[35]

Stewart likens American conservatives to the theocratic totalitarians of the Islamic world who, in keeping with sharia, treat women as chattel. "The American right," she said, "is certainly anti-woman, anti-inclusiveness, and I certainly oppose that here in my own country for my own sake, for my children's sake, for the way I want to live."

Embracing a particularly perverse moral relativism, Stewart argues that American society is at least as oppressive as societies governed by sharia. Left-wingers have been tricked into believing Muslim nations treat women badly, she contends.

The left has sort of been led down this primrose path—and I have to think it's media-and-government-orchestrated—into

---

[33] "All aboard! Obama pals back violent Gaza flotilla," by Aaron Klein, WND, May 31, 2010, http://www.wnd.com/2010/05/160661/, accessed June 3, 2016. HAMAS is an acronym that stands for Ḥarakat al-Muqāwamah al-ʾIslāmiyyah, or in English, Islamic Resistance Movement.

[34] "Counter-Intelligent: The surveillance and indictment of Lynne Stewart (an interview)," by Susie Day, Monthly Review, November 2002, monthlyreview.org/2002/11/01/counter-intelligent/, accessed May 15, 2016

[35] "Slapping Lynne Stewart on the wrist," by Matthew Vadum, *Human Events*, Oct. 23, 2006, http://humanevents.com/2006/10/23/slapping-lynne-stewart-on-the-wrist/

saying, "Oh, those Islamists, they do terrible things to women! So therefore, we can't support them." But actually, we do terrible things to women here too. [...] Part of the way that they are able to debunk Islam is to use over and over and over the women issue. So unless they intend to make equal pay for women and not quibble over Title Nine and all the other things they do in this country, I find that it's sort of the pot calling the kettle black.[36]

Anything that threatens the progress of Islamic supremacism is bad, according to Stewart.

The Global War on Terror is racist and fraudulent, she said in 2013. "Keep the populace terrorized so that they look to Big Brother Government for protection. Cannon fodder for the 'throwaways' in our society — young, poor, uneducated, persons of color."[37]

American Communist activist Yuri Kochiyama saw no contradiction between her Marxism and her embrace of Islam. She was a close friend of Malcolm X and converted to Islam. She even praised Osama bin Laden in the aftermath of 9/11.

To me, [bin Laden] is in the category of Malcolm X, Che Guevara, Patrice Lumumba, Fidel Castro, all leaders that I admire. They had much in common. Besides being strong leaders who brought consciousness to their people, they all had severe dislike for the U.S. government and those who held power in the U.S. I think all of them felt the U.S. government and its spokesmen were all arrogant, racist, hypocritical, self-righteous, and power hungry ... I thank Islam for bin Laden. America's greed, aggressiveness, and self-righteous arrogance must be stopped.[38]

British communist Chris Harman said the Left should not view Muslims as "our prime enemies" because "[t]hey are not responsible for the system of

---

[36] "Exclusive Interview: Lynne Stewart," by Bill Weinberg, *World War 3 Report*, June 30, 2002, ww4report.com/static/40.html#stewart, accessed May 15, 2016

[37] "The Persecution of Lynne Stewart," by Chris Hedges, Truth Dig, April 23, 2013, www.truthdig.com/report/item/the_persecution_of_lynne_stewart_20130421, accessed May 15, 2016

[38] "Google honors pro-Osama bin Laden radical with doodle," by Phil Shiver, Conservative Review, May 19, 2016, https://www.conservativereview.com/commentary/2016/05/google-honors-pro-osama-bin-laden-radical-with-doodle, accessed May 19, 2016

international capitalism." Their "feeling of revolt" should be "tapped for progressive purposes."[39]

Cooperating to undermine the U.S.

Leftist and Islamic supremacist political players around the world openly collaborate.

Venezuela's leftist strongman Hugo Chavez visited Iran in 2007. Of his alliance with Iranian President Mahmoud Ahmadinejad, he declared, "Here are two brother countries, united like a single fist."[40] Under Chavez, Venezuela allowed Hizballah, Iran's global terror proxy, and the Palestinian terrorist group HAMAS to open offices in the capital city Caracas.[41]

On a visit to Iran, Che Guevara's son, Camilo, gushed that his father would have "supported the country in its current struggle against the United States." Cuban dictator Fidel Castro visited the former Persia in 2001, boasting that "Iran and Cuba, in cooperation with each other, can bring America to its knees."[42]

In 2008, the Muslim Brotherhood front group, the Muslim Student Association at Northwestern University, invited leftist terrorists Bill Ayers and Bernardine Dohrn to speak at something called "Peaceful Progress: A Discourse on Affecting Change." Two years before that, Mohamed Elmasry of the Canadian Islamic Congress marveled at the Marxism-2006 conference in Toronto at how much could be achieved through the Muslim-leftist alliance. Perhaps unaware that the two sides working together wasn't a novel development, he said:

Now, for the first time in history, the political left is working with conservative Muslims on issues of social justice, with the long-term goal of building a world that lives by peace, through justice. Communists, Marxists, socialists, and nationalists are

---

[39] "'The Anti-Imperialism of Fools': A Cautionary Story on the Revolutionary Socialist Vanguard of England's Post-9/11 Anti-War Movement," by Camila Bassi. ACME: An International E-Journal for Critical Geographies, 2010, 9 (2): pp.128-9, http://shura.shu.ac.uk/1103/1/Bassi10.pdf, accessed May 15, 2016

[40] "Allied Menace," by Daniel Pipes, National Review, July 14, 2008, http://www.meforum.org/4502/the-islamist-leftist-allied-menace, accessed May 10, 2016

[41] "The Chavez Nightmare Comes To An End," by Matthew Vadum, FrontPageMag, March 5, 2013, http://www.frontpagemag.com/fpm/180204/chavez-nightmare-comes-end-matthew-vadum, accessed May 11, 2016

[42] "Allied Menace," by Daniel Pipes, National Review, July 14, 2008, http://www.meforum.org/4502/the-islamist-leftist-allied-menace, accessed May 10, 2016

working with civil libertarians, liberals, and conservatives to achieve this urgent goal together.[43]

"Red Ken" Livingstone, a Trotskyist former mayor of London, once "literally hugged prominent Islamist thinker Yusuf al-Qaradawi," writes Daniel Pipes. When he ran for president in 2004, former U.S. Rep. Dennis Kucinich (D-Ohio) led Muslims chanting "Allahu Akbar" ("God is great"), adding "I keep a copy of the Qur'an in my office." French philosopher Michel Foucault referred to Islamic Iran's founder and Supreme Leader Ayatollah Sayyid Ruhollah Musavi Khomeini as a "saint," only to be followed a year later by U.S. Ambassador to the United Nations Andrew Young who likewise said the man was "some kind of saint." German composer Karlheinz Stockhausen called the 9/11 attacks "the greatest work of art for the whole cosmos."[44]

During the Cold War, Muslims said they could work with the Soviet Union. "America is worse than Britain," Ayatollah Khomeini said in 1964, the year he was exiled from Iran. "Britain is worse than America and the Soviet Union is worse than both of them. Each one is worse than the other, each one is more abominable than the other. But today we are concerned with this malicious entity which is America."[45]

With the U.S.S.R. confined to the ash heap of history and Britain and much of Europe now increasingly sharia-compliant, the seeming odd bedfellows from radical domestic politics and Islamic supremacism are scheming to bring America to its knees.

---

[43] "The Left ♥ CAIR, MPAC, et al.," by Daniel Pipes, website of Daniel Pipes, Aug. 19, 2003, updated July 6, 2013, http://www.danielpipes.org/blog/2003/08/the-left-9829-cair-mpac-et-al, accessed May 9, 2016

[44] "Allied Menace," by Daniel Pipes, *National Review*, July 14, 2008, http://www.meforum.org/4502/the-islamist-leftist-allied-menace, accessed May 10, 2016

[45] "Allied Menace," by Daniel Pipes, *National Review*, July 14, 2008, http://www.meforum.org/4502/the-islamist-leftist-allied-menace, accessed May 10, 2016

CHAPTER 3

Lies, Grandstanding, and Sedition

A nd now a case study from 2016. The mangled bodies of Americans were still warm on the blood-stained nightclub floor when the Left launched a propaganda campaign to protect the totalitarian ideology of the Muslim terrorist who methodically slaughtered these innocents.

The jihadist bloodbath was carried out by Omar Mir Siddique Mateen at Pulse, a crowded gay dance club in Orlando, Fla. At least 49 victims died and 53 more were wounded in what has been called the worst mass shooting in American history and the worst terrorist attack on American soil since 9/11. Mateen, a U.S. citizen born to parents from Afghanistan, professed allegiance to the Islamic State and hailed the 2013 Boston Marathon bombers, the Kyrgyzstani-born ethnic Chechens, Tamerlan and Dzhokhar Tsarnaev, as his "homeboys" before police on the scene killed him. Islamic State corroborated the shooter's connection to it, reportedly claiming responsibility for the terrorist operation.

Although it was obvious almost from the beginning of the attack on June 12, 2016 to anyone following the news that this was an act of Islamic terrorism, the Left tried to seize control of the post-attack narrative. Veteran liberal journalist Tom Brokaw editorialized the real problem was *guns* not Islam. "Everything seems to get settled by a gun for whatever reasons," he said. The lies, knee-jerk reactions, and red herrings of TV talking heads like Brokaw were repeated over and over again by left-wingers all over the Internet and their allies in the media echo chamber.

U.S. Attorney General Loretta Lynch tried to whitewash Mateen's connection to Islam in appearances she made on Sunday morning TV talk shows on June 19. She explained why references to Islamic State to which Mateen pledged allegiance during a call to Orlando 9-1-1 while the attack was in progress, were going to be redacted in the soon-to-be-released transcript. This was obviously part of the Obama administration's public relations effort aimed at blaming guns, as opposed to a swaggering Muslim terrorist, for the shooting. "What we're not going to do is further proclaim this man's pledges of allegiance to terrorist groups, and further his propaganda," Lynch piously announced. After her remarks and the release of the bowdlerized transcript met with widespread condemnation and ridicule, the administration reversed itself the next day and released an accurate, unredacted transcript of the call. The government abandoned its previous position, claiming the redactions had "caused an unnecessary distraction from the hard work that the FBI and our law enforcement partners have been doing to investigate this heinous crime."[46]

In the hours and days after June 12, Democrat presidential candidate Hillary Clinton wasted no time blaming "radical jihadism" and "radical Islamism" for the attack. But this was unusual among leftists who were otherwise desperate to change the subject. Democrat lawmakers blamed inanimate firearms for the Muslim massacre. They staged a raucous "sit-in" in the House of Representatives on June 22 in an attempt to force a vote on expanded gun control measures. Journalists indulged the politicians by providing saturation media coverage of the stunt.

Shortly after the attack, President Barack Hussein Obama shrugged, claiming it was too early to know "the precise motivations of the killer." New York's leftist mayor, Bill de Blasio, blamed firearms, lamenting that "we have lost precious lives to the gun." Salon writer Amanda Marcotte blamed conservatives, Christians, and "the cult of toxic masculinity." Purported comedian John Fugelsang attacked gun rights, quipping that so many victims were killed rapidly because "in America, maniacs still have a God-given right to not have to reload mid-massacre." Edward Snowden enabler and gay activist Glenn Greenwald nonsensically huffed it was unfair to blame Islam because a "2015 Pew Poll found that U.S. Muslims were more accepting of homosexuality than evangelical Christians, Mormons and Jehovah's Witnesses." ACLU staff attorney Chase Strangio blamed conservative Christians for their "thoughts and prayers and Islamophobia" that "created this anti-queer climate." After complaining about the "systematic violence" Christians, Republicans, and Democrats have subjected "queer people to," gay activist Steven W. Thrasher lectured that "We should remember not to blame all members of any other religion or political ideology for what one person does."[47]

Islam scholar Robert Spencer rejects Thrasher's reasoning:

The problem is that any examination of the motives and goals of people such as Omar Mateen, and any consideration of what can be done about them, is always met with the accusation that such examinations and considerations constitute blaming all Muslims for the actions of jihadis. It is

---

[46] "DOJ Reversal: Unredacted Transcripts of Orlando Gunman's 9-1-1 Call Released After Outrage Over Initially Scrubbed Documents," Fox News website, June 20, 2016, http://nation.foxnews.com/2016/06/20/doj-scrub-islam-references-transcripts-orlando-terrorists-calls-police

[47] "Ramadan Massacre in Orlando," by Robert Spencer, FrontPageMag, June 13, 2016, http://www.frontpagemag.com/fpm/263161/ramadan-massacre-orlando-robert-spencer, accessed June 13, 2016

so obviously fallacious that it is hard not to suspect that it is an intentional obfuscation.

The Qur'an doesn't just express disapproval of homosexuality — it requires gays to be killed, Spencer writes. President Obama refused to acknowledge this motive for the attack, some would say in keeping with his oft-displayed reverence for Islam. Doing so would have required him to justify Islamic teachings about gays. Spencer continues:

> **The Qur'an says: "If two men among you are guilty of lewdness, punish them both. If they repent and amend, leave them alone; for Allah is Oft-returning, Most Merciful." (4:16) That seems rather mild, but there's more. The Qur'an also depicts Allah raining down stones upon people for engaging in homosexual activity: "We also sent Lot. He said to his people: "Do you commit lewdness such as no people in creation committed before you? For you practice your lusts on men in preference to women: you are indeed a people transgressing beyond bounds. ... And we rained down on them a shower of brimstone: Then see what was the end of those who indulged in sin and crime!" (7:80)**

Judging from gays' growing post-Orlando interest in availing themselves of their Second Amendment rights, they would seem to agree more with Spencer than Thrasher.

The Left Sides with Osama bin Laden and Mahmoud Ahmadinejad

As I suggested earlier, that jihadists and leftists are natural allies is counterintuitive to many.

As former leftist David Horowitz observes, the two sides are willing to work together to try to make their ultimately doomed marriage work. The Left abhors the United States and its market-based economy so much that it is willing to link arms with Islam, "which emphatically and unambiguously rejects virtually everything for which the socialist left claims to stand: the peaceful resolution of international conflict; respect and tolerance for other cultures and faiths; civil liberties; freedom of expression; freedom of thought; human rights; democracy; women's rights; gay rights; and the separation of church and state."[48]

---

[48] "Radical Islam's alliance with the socialist left," by David Horowitz, date unknown, Discover the Networks, http://www.discoverthenetworks.org/viewSubCategory.asp?id=291, accessed May 22, 2016

Al-Qa'eda leader Osama bin Laden laid out his case against America to CNN in 1997. "We declared jihad against the U.S. government because the U.S. government is unjust, criminal and tyrannical."

After listing various complaints against the United States, bin Laden said:

> **For this and other acts of aggression and injustice, we have declared jihad against the U.S., because in our religion it is our duty to make jihad so that God's word is the one exalted to the heights and so that we drive the Americans away from all Muslim countries ... the American people, they are not exonerated from responsibility, because they chose this government and voted for it despite their knowledge of its crimes in Palestine, Lebanon, Iraq and in other places and its support of its agent regimes who filled our prisons with our best children and scholars.[49]**

Just as the devout Muslim seeks to create an Islamic paradise on earth, the leftist seeks to abolish or at least impose crippling restrictions on capitalism in hopes of creating a utopian society. Horowitz continues:

> **Central to both radical Islam and the radical Western left is an inclination to overthrow the existing order by any means necessary, so as to create a paradise on earth. Leftists may find the bigotry and intolerance of Islamic radicals repugnant, but their desire to rid the world of U.S. "imperialism" and capitalism overrides this revulsion and beckons them to forge the unholy alliance.**

Just as left-wingers have been known to swoon over anti-American mass murderers like Ernesto "Che" Guevara, they romanticize jihadis, seeing goodness and benevolent intentions where they do not exist.

This willful naivety was on display six years earlier when more than 100 progressive activists, led by former U.S. Attorney General Ramsey Clark and former U.S. Rep. Cynthia McKinney (D-Ga.), sat down for a meal with Iran's president at the time, Mahmoud Ahmadinejad. They said they wanted to express their support for his stand against American imperialism. These starry-eyed leftists didn't mind that Iranian politicians call the United States the "Great Satan" (Israel is called the "Little Satan") or that Ahmadinejad

---

[49] "Transcript Of Osama Bin Ladin Interview By Peter Arnett," Information Clearing House website, date unknown, http://www.informationclearinghouse.info/article7204.htm, accessed Sept. 20, 2016

himself is a Jew-hating Holocaust denier who has publicly claimed that there are no homosexuals in his country (perhaps on the premise that as soon as they are discovered they are tried and executed). It didn't trouble the left-wingers that he may have personally participated in the taking of 52 Americans as hostages for 444 days after Iranian revolutionaries stormed the U.S. embassy in Tehran in 1979. Nor did they object to the fact that the Islamic Republic of Iran is the world's leading state sponsor of terrorism and that it is a country that puts homosexuals, adulterers, and religious dissenters to death, in obedience to Islamic Law.

His postprandial address did not disappoint the assembled social justice warriors. Discussing his country's relationship with the United States, he said "we believe that the only element that can lead to viable peace is to carry out justice – without justice, peace is meaningless," he said, paraphrasing the "no justice, no peace," mantra of the Los Angeles rioters in 1992. He added that "trying to build peace is the most important and comprehensive struggle that mankind can have." Of course, almost certainly unbeknownst to his dinner guests, the actual meaning of "justice" in the Islamic context is "sharia" and only sharia, while "peace" refers to the peace of a world subjugated entirely to sharia by means of "struggle" (*i.e.,* jihad). They are using the same language but with entirely different meaning.

Markets are to blame for strife in the world, Ahmadinejad said. Echoing a speech he made at the United Nations earlier that day, he continued, "It seems to me that one of the main factors in discrimination, and war, and injustice, is the capitalist system. The foundation of the capitalist system is based on superiority, hegemony, and the violation of the rights of others. You can see they start wars to fill up their pockets."[50]

Other radicals in attendance that night were: MOVE "minister of information" Ramona Africa; activist Amiri Baraka whose poem "Somebody Blew Up America?" accused Israel of involvement in the 9/11 attacks; Don DeBar of WBAIx.org; Sarah Flounders, co-director of International Action Center; Rev. Graylan Hagler of Plymouth Congregational United Church of Christ in Washington, D.C.; Larry Holmes of Bail Out the People Movement; Ryme Katkhouda of the People's Media Center; Shafeah M'balia of Black Workers for Justice; Michael McPhearson of United for Peace and Justice; Ardeshir and Eleanor Ommani, co-founders of the American-Iranian Friendship Committee; Million Worker March Movement organizer Brenda

[50] "My dinner with Mahmoud Ahmadinejad," by Norman Stockwell, AlterNet, Sept. 25, 2010, http://www.alternet.org/story/148300/my_dinner_with_mahmoud_ahmadinejad, accessed May 11, 2016

Stokely; and Phil Wilayto of Virginia Defenders for Freedom, Justice and Equality.[51]

Another attendee described how her fellow leftists fawned over Ahmadinejad.

One after another, the guests at the dinner delivered prepared statements, posing no questions or challenges to the Iranian delegation. Mostly, people expressed outrage over U.S. foreign policy. They lauded Ahmadinejad as a hero for standing up to the bullying of the United States government and likened the meeting to Malcolm X's encounters in Africa with revolutionaries fighting against colonialism. Many apologized for decades of dire U.S. policy towards Iran, while calling for self-determination for Iran and confidence in Ahmadinejad.[52]

During the same trip to the Big Apple, Ahmadinejad secretly met with Nation of Islam leader Louis Farrakhan and members of the New Black Panther Party. Farrakhan traveled to Libya in 1984 with President Obama's America-hating pastor, Jeremiah Wright, to meet then-dictator Muammar Qaddafi.[53]

Left-wing Islamic Politicians: Obama, Ellison, Carson

Leftists sympathetic to Islam hold elective office at the national level in the U.S. and do not view left-wing radicalism and Islam as in conflict.

Moreover, jihadists and their supporters lie and they don't feel bad about it. Just as Saul Alinsky adherents justify lying to advance the leftist cause, Muslims embrace *taqiyya*, a doctrine that allows Muslims to lie to non-Muslims "above and beyond the context of 'self-preservation.'" As Dr. Sami Mukaram, a former Islamic studies professor at the American University of Beirut who wrote some 25 books on Islam explains:

---

[51] "Iranian President Mahmoud Ahmadinejad Meets Activists, Journalists," by Abayomi Azikiwe, Pan-African News Wire, Sept. 28, 2010, http://panafricannews.blogspot.com/2010/09/iranian-president-mahmoud-ahmadinejad.html, accessed May 11, 2016

[52] "Admiring Ahmadinejad and overlooking activists: we're better than this," by Bitta Mostofi, Common Dreams, Oct. 15, 2010, http://www.commondreams.org/views/2010/10/15/admiring-ahmadinejad-and-overlooking-activists-were-better, accessed May 11, 2016

[53] "Ahmadinejad, Black Panthers & Farrakhan hold 'secret' NY rendezvous," by Meredith Jessup, The Blaze, Sept. 26, 2010, http://www.theblaze.com/stories/2010/09/26/ahmadinejad-black-panthers-farrakhan-hold-secret-ny-rendezvous/, accessed May 11, 2016

Taqiyya is of fundamental importance in Islam. Practically every Islamic sect agrees to it and practices it ... We can go so far as to say that the practice of *taqiyya* is mainstream in Islam, and that those few sects not practicing it diverge from the mainstream ... *Taqiyya* is very prevalent in Islamic politics, especially in the modern era.[54]

American politicians also practice *taqiyya*.

Although some Americans might cringe at the thought of categorizing President Obama, probably America's most radically left-wing chief executive ever, as a jihad supporter, his policies in office arguably did much to advance the jihadist cause. Obama used to make little effort to conceal his radical associations. For 20 years Obama worshipped at Jeremiah Wright's hateful, unabashedly anti-American Trinity United Church of Christ, a hotbed of black liberation theology. In October 1995, Obama considered his participation in Nation of Islam leader Louis Farrakhan's Million Man March to be so important that he took precious time off from his campaign for the Illinois Senate to go to Washington, D.C., with Wright. Farrakhan, who has called Obama the new "messiah," calls Jews "bloodsuckers" and "satanic." He is also close to Obama, academic Vibert White Jr., formerly a senior officer in Nation of Islam, said in 2008. For many years, the two men have had "an open line between them" to talk about policy and strategy, either directly or through intermediaries. "Remember that for years, if you were a politician in Chicago, you had to have some type of relationship with Louis Farrakhan. You had to. If you didn't, you would be ostracized out of black Chicago," White said.[55]

Obama backed the now-deposed Muslim Brotherhood president of Egypt, Mohamed Morsi, and with then-Secretary of State Hillary Clinton's help, set fire to the Middle East and North Africa during the catastrophic so-called Arab Spring of 2011. Obama and Hillary Clinton both sat idly by on the eleventh anniversary of 9/11 and allowed U.S. Ambassador to Libya J. Christopher Stevens, information officer Sean Smith, and former Navy SEALS Glen Doherty and Tyrone S. Woods to be killed by jihadists at the

---

[54] "Taqiyya about taqiyya," by Raymond Ibrahim, FrontPageMag, April 10, 2014, http://www.frontpagemag.com/fpm/223141/taqiyya-about-taqiyya-raymond-ibrahim, accessed May 19, 2016. A related doctrine in Islam is tawriya which "allows Muslims to lie in virtually all circumstances provided that the lie is articulated in a way that it is technically true," Ibrahim writes. If a person says "I do not have a penny in my pocket," most people will assume the person has no money on him. Under *tawriya* the person may actually have dollar bills in his possession but is not considered to be lying by claiming to be pennyless.

[55] "Obama-Farrakhan Ties Are Close, Ex-Aide Says," Newsmax, Nov. 3, 2008, http://www.newsmax.com/InsideCover/farrakhan-obama-islam/2008/11/03/id/326298/, accessed May 19, 2016

U.S. mission in Benghazi, Libya. Whenever there is a jihadist attack in the U.S., as for example the Fort Hood massacre of 2009, Obama tended to downplay any connection to Islamic inspiration, refusing to label it Islamic terrorism (and unfortunately, until U.S. law is changed to permit a jihadist label for someone without demonstrable connections to any of the groups listed on the Department of State's Foreign Terrorist Organizations list, this is the way it will remain). He wants to shut down the terrorist detention facility in Guantanamo Bay, Cuba, and released dangerous terrorists from there at a furious pace in his effort to close the facility, allowing many of them to return to the battlefield. In 2014, Obama swapped U.S. Army Sgt. Bowe Bergdahl, a deserter alleged to have collaborated with the Taliban-aligned Haqqani network, for five senior Taliban operatives. In nuclear talks with the Iranian regime, he eventually (July 2015) concluded a deal whose terms, unless reversed, demonstrably will help the apocalyptic mullahs of Iran obtain nuclear weapons through a loophole-ridden nuclear deal that no one has actually signed.

Muslim lawmakers Reps. Keith Ellison (D-Minn.) and Andre Carson (D-Ind.) are both practicing Muslims who frequently accuse the United states of bigotry towards Muslims. Both men have extensive links with Muslim Brotherhood front groups in the U.S.

Ellison is co-chairman of the far-left Congressional Progressive Caucus and was nominated to be the new Chairman of the Democratic National Committee (DNC). A longtime supporter of Nation of Islam who may actually have been a member of the radical group, he blames America for Muslim terrorism. In 2009, he said that "violent extremism with a Muslim veneer is essentially a post-colonial reaction" (*i.e.,* a reaction to Western colonialism of the past) and a manifestation of a "political environment rooted in grievance." Ellison is a regular at events sponsored by HAMAS-doing-business-as the Council on American-Islamic Relations (CAIR) and the Islamic Society of North America (ISNA), two groups the U.S. Department of Justice has identified as co-conspirators in the Holy Land Foundation HAMAS terror funding trial, the largest such trial ever prosecuted in the U.S.[56]

Carson believes the ends justify the means. He hurled a false racism charge at the Tea Party movement at the height of the Obamacare debate in Congress. Carson flat out lied, saying that on March 20, 2010, Obamacare opponents in a crowd outside the U.S. Capitol shouted the N-word "fifteen times" while Rep. John Lewis (D-Ga.) walked by. The late Andrew Breitbart put up a $100,000 reward for video and audio evidence that the event

---

[56] "Rep. Keith Ellison: apologist for jihad," by Matthew Vadum, FrontPageMag, Feb. 22, 2015, http://www.frontpagemag.com/fpm/251881/rep-keith-ellison-apologist-jihad-matthew-vadum

happened. No one claimed the reward.[57] In January 2015, Rep. Carson was named to the House Permanent Select Committee on Intelligence by the Democratic Leader of the House, Nancy Pelosi.[58]

Ellison and Carson worked together in an effort to silence a prominent international critic of Islam. The two lawmakers argued that Dutch Member of Parliament and Freedom Party leader Geert Wilders was a dangerous Islamophobe and asked federal agencies to prevent him from visiting the country. To that end, they wrote to Homeland Security Secretary Jeh Johnson and Secretary of State John Kerry in 2015. "We should not be importing hate speech," they wrote. The government should "deny Mr. Wilders entry due to his participation in inciting anti-Muslim aggression and violence." In the past, the U.S. has denied entry "to a foreign leader who is responsible for severe violations of religious freedom," so there is a precedent for blocking Wilders, they argued. Wilders may have strong views that he forcefully expresses, but he's no lynch mob leader. "I don't know what Islamophobia is," Wilders said during the Capitol Hill visit Ellison and Carson failed to block. "I read the letter from the two congressmen and it was full of, it raised a lot of nonsense. They said that I was guilty of incitement of violence and things like that. It was full of really crazy stuff."[59]

[57] "No more beer summits," by Andrew Breitbart, Breitbart News, April 26, 2010, http://www.breitbart.com/big-government/2010/04/26/no-more-beer-summits--tea-party-n-word-incident-didnt-happen--and-the-congressional-black-caucus-owes-america-an-apology/, accessed May 19, 2016

[58] "Carson Appointed to House Intelligence Committee," January 14, 2015. https://carson.house.gov/media-center/press-releases/carson-appointed-to-house-intelligence-committee

[59] "Geert Wilders: I Won't Stop Warning the West About Islam," by Matthew Vadum, FrontPageMag, May 4, 2015, http://www.frontpagemag.com/fpm/256238/geert-wilders-i-wont-stop-warning-west-about-islam-matthew-vadum

CHAPTER 4

'Islamophobia' and Working the System for Jihad

Jihadis and their leftist allies in the U.S. use the country's open democratic system to wage war against America. They conduct psychological operations against the American public to raise doubts about who the nation's enemies really are. They have the news media and those left-wing think tanks known as universities in their pocket. They think they are untouchable, and to an extent, they are.

Whenever a politician names the Islamic supremacist enemy, that person is subjected to a barrage of hate from politically correct elitists who stand ready to smear on a moment's notice. The public servant is ridiculed as a racist even though Islam is not a race and portrayed as a xenophobic kook who can't let go of America's past. Ask former Rep. Michele Bachmann (R-Minn.) and current Reps. Louie Gohmert (R-Texas) and Steve King (R-Iowa).

In the U.S., U.K., Canada and elsewhere, the media-academic-entertainment complex largely sanitizes Islam, presenting it as a benign, misunderstood religion. Knowing next to nothing about Islamic doctrine, history, law or scripture, they lash out at those who document the medieval brutality of sharia, the oppression of women, and the persecution of homosexuals under Islamic Law.

To them, "Islamophobia" explains why the U.S. incarcerates Muslim terrorists.

"I am convinced that Gitmo and other places like Gitmo only exist because its detainees are Muslims," former Center for Constitutional Rights president Michael Ratner said in 2012. "I can't imagine a Christian Gitmo. I cannot imagine a Jewish Guantanamo. It exists because of Islamophobia."[60]

Ratner was an adjunct law professor at Columbia University and served as special counsel to Haitian President Jean-Bertrand Aristide, a Marxist who was overthrown in 2004. Ratner wrote in his 1997 book, *Che Guevara and the FBI: The U.S. Political Police Dossier on the Latin American Revolutionary*, that "it was Che Guevara, more than any other figure, who embodied both [the Cuban] revolution and solidarity with peoples fighting to be free from U.S. hegemony."

The extreme-left Center for Constitutional Rights, by the way, helped to give America's terrorist enemies access to the U.S. civilian justice system.

---

[60] "A leftist's harsh words for the unholy alliance," by Matthew Vadum, FrontPageMag, July 11, 2013, http://www.frontpagemag.com/fpm/195918

The Center scored a major legal victory in 2004 when the Supreme Court ruled 6-3 in *Rasul v. Bush* that its clients, 16 foreign nationals captured during U.S. hostilities with the Taliban in Afghanistan, had the legal right to challenge their detentions in U.S. civilian courts. To assist in CCR's legal campaign, the Atlantic Philanthropies gave it $2.25 million. The Ford Foundation gave CCR $200,000 to advocate for the due-process rights of Guantanamo prisoners.

Groups suspected of ties to Islamic terrorists have also donated to CCR. Two organizations in Virginia, Safa Trust Inc. and the IIIT, each gave CCR donations of up to $99,999 in 2005. Federal agents investigating terrorist financing raided the offices of both organizations in 2002. The Ohio branch of the Council on American-Islamic Relations (CAIR), gave CCR up to $2,499 in 2005. In 2005 CAIR gave Ratner its Civil Rights Award.[61]

The Center for Constitutional Rights is just one of many radical activist groups using our tax laws against us. "By far the most important tactic utilized by terrorist groups in America has been to use non-profit organizations to establish a zone of legitimacy within which fund-raising, recruitment, and even outright planning can occur," Steven Emerson of the Investigative Project on Terrorism has said.

America itself has become "a primary base of Islamic terrorist operations," David Horowitz observes.

America has functioned as a prime organizing site for international terrorism because the liberties provided by the American legal system allow terrorists to travel freely, raise money, propagandize, recruit, and move men and money across international borders. Terrorist organizers, including the leaders of al Qaeda, Hamas and the Muslim Brotherhood have all traveled extensively in the United States, raised funds, recruited soldiers and sent emissaries back and forth across America's borders. This makes control of borders and other immigration issues a crucial front in the anti-terrorist war.[62]

---

[61] "The Terrorists' Legal Team: Case by Case, the Center for Constitutional Rights Undermines America," by Matthew Vadum, *Organization Trends*, September 2006, https://capitalresearch.org/2006/09/the-terrorists-legal-team-case-by-case-the-center-for-constitutional-rights-undermines-america/, accessed May 1, 2016. An interesting historical footnote: Rachel Meeropol, senior staff attorney at CCR, is a granddaughter of Julius and Ethel Rosenberg, who were executed in 1953 for passing secrets of the atomic bomb to the Soviet Union.

[62] "Unholy Alliance: How the Left Supports the Terrorists at Home," by David Horowitz, FrontPageMag, Sept. 24, 2004, http://archive.frontpagemag.com/readArticle.aspx?ARTID=11263, accessed May 3, 2016

Language is a critical tool in the arsenal of those who wish to fundamentally transform the United States of America. The thinking is that making it difficult to express opposition to A is likely to contribute to the flourishing of A. The Left has long understood this, swatting down dissent by intimidation, smears, and name-calling.

Criticism of Muslims for virtually any reason is often met with hysterical shrieks and verbal abuse from affective left-wingers perpetually on hair-trigger outrage alert. So an invented concept called "Islamophobia" has become a key weapon in the Islamic-leftist war for hearts and minds.

"Islamophobia," a deliberately vague conceptual vessel into which meaning may be poured, is wielded as a cudgel against those who oppose Islamic supremacism, sharia, and jihad as well as those who are merely skeptical of them. The idea is to eventually make it as difficult and uncomfortable as possible to criticize the belief system founded by Muhammad in the 7th century after the birth of Christ. And there are a lot of well-heeled funders who are part of a long-term campaign aimed at mainstreaming the tenets of Islam in American society.

Americans' respect for civil rights and political correctness are weapons of infiltration used by our Islamic supremacist enemies. Just like our Soviet Communist enemies during the Cold War, Muslims are using Americans' goodness and their sense of fair play, including an aversion to being accused of racial stereotyping, against America. Islam is not a race, of course, but smears don't necessarily have to make sense.

Accusing people of Islamophobia is a PC stratagem aimed at discrediting and silencing those critics. Supporters of Islam in the U.S. frequently hurl the epithet "Islamophobe" to shut down debate, about, well, anything. The smear is used against both critics of Islam and those who merely question whether it is the religion of peace the dangerously nonjudgmental Left assures Americans it is. But in the real world, if one fears Islamic ideology as an imperialist, totalitarian force, one is rational. "Phobia" implies that one who harbors such fears or is skeptical of the intentions of Muslims is mentally unbalanced.

There are differing accounts of the etymology of Islamophobia. French author Pascal Bruckner wrote that "Iranian fundamentalists" invented the word in the late 1970s "in analogy to 'xenophobia'" and "to silence those Muslims who question the Koran and who demand equality of the sexes." The purpose "of this word was to declare Islam inviolate. Whoever crosses this border is deemed a racist. This term, which is worthy of totalitarian propaganda, is deliberately unspecific about whether it refers to a religion, a belief system or its faithful adherent around the world."[63] Feminist Meredith

---

[63] "The invention of Islamophobia," by Pascal Bruckner, Sign and Sight, Jan. 3, 2011, http://www.signandsight.com/features/2123.html, accessed May 6, 2016

Tax states that French sources "attribute it to Ayatollah Khomeini, who said Iranian women who rejected the veil were 'Islamophobic.'"[64]

The anti-Islamophobia movement is built on "foundations created by progressives and, as a result, is already well advanced in the West," David Horowitz and Robert Spencer explain:

> **In 1996 the Runnymede Trust, a leftist group in England, established a "Commission on British Muslims and Islamophobia." Its elaborate definition of Islamophobia has since become a model for Muslim Brotherhood fronts like CAIR and the Muslim Students Association in their drive to impose anti-Islamophobia strictures on everyone and suppress critics of the Islamic jihad. Under the Runnymede definition, Islamophobia includes any one of these eight components:**
>
> 1. **"Islam seen as a single monolithic bloc, static and unresponsive to new realities.**
> 2. **Islam seen as separate and other – (a) not having any aims or values in common with other cultures (b) not affected by them (c) not influencing them.**
> 3. **Islam seen as inferior to the West – barbaric, irrational, primitive, sexist.**
> 4. **Islam seen as violent, aggressive, threatening, supportive of terrorism, engaged in 'a clash of civilizations'.**
> 5. **Islam seen as a political ideology, used for political or military advantage.**
> 6. **Criticisms made by Islam of 'the West' rejected out of hand.**
> 7. **Hostility towards Islam used to justify discriminatory practices towards Muslims and exclusion of Muslims from mainstream society.**
> 8. **Anti-Muslim hostility accepted as natural and 'normal'."**

According to Claire Berlinski, it surfaced in the 1990s. "The neologism 'Islamophobia,' did not simply emerge *ex nihilo*. It was invented, deliberately,

---

[64] "A leftist's harsh words for the unholy alliance," by Matthew Vadum, FrontPageMag, July 11, 2013, http://www.frontpagemag.com/fpm/195918

by a Muslim Brotherhood front organization, the International Institute for Islamic Thought, which is based in Northern Virginia."

Abdur-Rahman Muhammad, a former member of the IIIT who has since denounced the group, was an eyewitness to the birth of the word. "This loathsome term," he writes, "is nothing more than a thought-terminating cliché conceived in the bowels of Muslim think tanks for the purpose of beating down critics." It was coined "to silence critics of political Islam" and enable Muslims to be portrayed as victims. The coiners opted to follow the example of gay activists who threw the word "homophobia" around to "beat up their critics."[65]

Regardless of who thought it up first, the way the term is used today resembles the way the phrase "thought crime" was used in George Orwell's great dystopian novel, *Nineteen Eighty-Four*. As Horowitz and Spencer explain, in that novel "written at the height of the Cold War, citizens are watched by a secret police for 'thought crimes' committed against the totalitarian state. These thought crimes are simply attitudes and ideas the authorities regard as politically incorrect."

Islamophobia refers "to a modern-day thought crime," they write. The purpose of the *-phobia* suffix "is to suggest that any fear associated with Islam is irrational – whether that fear stems from the fact that its prophet and current-day imams call on believers to kill infidels, or because the attacks of 9/11 were carried out to implement those calls. Worse than that, it is to suggest that such a response to those attacks reflects a bigotry that itself should be feared."[66]

It's time for another case study

Remember October 2010, when mass hysteria broke out at National Public Radio? Panic ensued when liberal commentator Juan Williams dared to share a personal anecdote on "The O'Reilly Factor" on Fox News Channel.

NPR fired Williams not because he disparaged Muslims – he didn't — but because he made the impolitic admission that he becomes "nervous" and "worried" when he sees people in "Muslim garb" on airplanes. He experienced an emotion and talked about it on television. And he's not the only American who gets a little bit jittery in such situations in a country where Islamic terrorists killed 3,000 Americans on 9/11 by flying commercial jetliners into the World Trade Center, Pentagon, and a field in Pennsylvania.

---

[65] "Moderate Muslim Watch: How the Term 'Islamophobia' Got Shoved Down Your Throat," by Claire Berlinski, Ricochet, Nov. 24, 2010, https://ricochet.com/archives/moderate-muslim-watch-how-the-term-islamophobia-got-shoved-down-your-throat/, accessed May 15, 2016

[66] "Islamophobia: Thought Crime of the Totalitarian Future," by David Horowitz and Robert Spencer, 2011, David Horowitz Freedom Center, available at http://www.discoverthenetworks.org/Articles/Islamophobia.pdf, accessed May 6, 2016

Williams and others experiencing the same anxieties aren't bad people. They're not bigots. They can't control their emotional reactions to stimuli. They're just normal, rational human beings and the fear they experience has at least some basis in reality.

But in the world of political correctness, that's no excuse.

Williams was cashiered because his comments were perceived by the cloistered mandarins of public radio as "Islamophobic." NPR believed Williams thought bad thoughts; he should have felt ashamed by his authentic psychological reflexes and he definitely should not have admitted these thought crimes on TV.

Whether the fear of which Williams spoke was well-founded or reasonable is irrelevant. The political correctness that has metastasized in American culture requires that no one speak ill of Islam or say anything that might stigmatize or *other-ize* a Muslim in any way. All Americans must think and say only nice things about Islam even though its adherents have been slaughtering, subjugating, and enslaving people for nearly 1,400 years. This is not to make the gross generalization that all Muslims are bad people but it is surely understatement to say that Islam has a bad track record.

But the friends of Islam don't believe in the marketplace of ideas. They are determined to stamp out critical thinking, and they have an army of nonprofit organizations, foundations, academics, media outlets, and shrieking name-calling activists to help them.

This is not, by the way some abstract academic discussion. Working through the Organization for Islamic Cooperation (formerly the Organization of the Islamic Conference), Islamic states have been trying for years to convince the United Nations to criminalize this thought crime they call Islamophobia.

The OIC claims to support freedom of speech but at the same time holds that freedom of speech does not include the freedom to blaspheme or insult Islam. All Muslim majority countries "already have some sort of Islamic blasphemy codes, whether formal or informal," notes attorney and commentator Deborah Weiss. But OIC leaders are calculating. If they openly demanded Islamic blasphemy laws in Western countries, the non-Muslim world would balk. Instead the OIC "uses multi-lateral conferences, 'consensus building' and legal instruments such as UN resolutions, with language more palatable to free societies, in order to achieve its goals gradually and incrementally."[67]

---

[67] "The Organization of Islamic Cooperation's Jihad on Free Speech, by Deborah Weiss, Center for Security Policy website, June 6, 2015, pp.16-17, https://www.centerforsecuritypolicy.org/wp-content/uploads/2015/07/OIC_Free_Speech_Jihad.pdf, accessed May 9, 2016

And, as noted earlier, the Obama administration hasn't exactly been burning up the long-distance telephone lines trying to change the minds of the OIC member-states. Delete

Meanwhile, academics have been hard at work trying to cement the idea of Islamophobia in popular consciousness. The Center for Race and Gender at the University of California at Berkeley publishes its own magazine to follow developments in this invented discipline. A recent edition of the *Islamophobia Studies Journal* posits that the United States is a massive jail and that the Muslims within it are inmates.

[T]he way to evaluate and approach the American Muslim community in the current period should be approached within a prison-prisoner lens. Here, the ability to move around and enjoy privileges should not be confused with freedom, equality, constitutional rights, and dignity in the full sense of the word. Let us be honest for a moment and detail the Muslim predicament in today's America: a community subject to structured governmental control, surveillance, entrapment schemes, guilt by association, and punitive measures instituted to elicit "correct" conduct and proper political and religious speech.

Its editors complain about legitimate government efforts to combat Islamic terrorism, using Americans' reverence for religious liberty to distract from Muslims' involvement in subversive activities. The "levels of intrusion into Muslim religious space, whereby the government admits to deploying informants and monitoring leaders within these institutions" is unacceptable to them. In fact, any effort to combat Islamic terror is unacceptable to these people. The Countering Violent Extremism (CVE) program in the U.S. and Prevent in Britain "are symptoms of the prison-prisoner relationship," they claim.[68]

Education officials elsewhere have been taking their cues from the White House.

Throughout his presidency, Barack Obama, who has described the Muslim call to prayer as "one of the prettiest sounds on earth at sunset," seemed obsessed with boosting self-esteem in the most backward countries on the planet. The president even made the space agency NASA into a Muslim outreach organization.

NASA chief Charles Bolden told Al-Jazeera in 2010 that he was tasked "to find a way to reach out to the Muslim world and engage much more with

---

[68] *Islamophobia Studies Journal*, Fall 2015, Volume 3, Issue 1, http://crg.berkeley.edu/sites/default/files/IS%20Journal%20-%20Fall2015.pdf, accessed June 11, 2016

dominantly Muslim nations to help them feel good about their historic contribution to science, math and engineering."

This kind of indoctrination is legion. Universities, think tanks, and media outlets are armed to the teeth with Islamic propaganda, some of which is funded by U.S. taxpayers and Islamic supremacists overseas. There is concern as well that public school teaching plans in Tennessee and other states are already being based on these heavily biased, anti-American materials.

Islamophile Carl W. Ernst, Kenan Distinguished Professor at the University of North Carolina at Chapel Hill, provides a resource page on so-called Islamophobia on his taxpayer-supported website. It encourages readers to gorge themselves on self-serving drivel from the far-left Southern Poverty Law Center and the Center for American Progress. It refers readers to the Bridge Initiative: A Research Project on Islamophobia at the Prince Alwaleed bin Talal Center for Muslim-Christian Understanding at Georgetown University and the Islamophobia Research & Documentation Project at the University of California, Berkeley. At Berkeley, the Institute for South Asia Studies offers "K-14" lesson plans.[69]

Resources for combating so-called Islamophobia abound on the Internet. There is the University of Pittsburgh-based three-state Consortium for Educational Resources on Islamic Studies (CERIS). There is the United Nations Educational, Scientific and Cultural Organization (UNESCO) booklet, "Guidelines for Educators on Countering Intolerance and Discrimination against Muslims: Addressing Islamophobia through Education." There is the Middle East Institute at Columbia University. There is "Teaching Tolerance," a project of the Southern Poverty Law Center. There is the teacher guide, "Islam in Asia: People, Practices, Tradition," put out jointly by the University of Washington and the Seattle Times. Portland State University provides "Middle East Teaching Tools: Resources for Educators," which is intended "to support education about the Middle East at the K-12 level." There are resource pages on the website of Harvard University's Center for Middle Eastern Studies and on the websites of many other institutions of higher learning.[70]

---

[69] Institute for South Asia Studies, UC Berkeley. http://southasia.berkeley.edu/

[70] "CAIR demands Muslim indoctrination of 12-year-olds," by Matthew Vadum, FrontPageMag, Oct. 16, 2015, http://www.frontpagemag.com/fpm/260466/cair-demands-muslim-indoctrination-12-year-olds-matthew-vadum

CHAPTER 5
Weaponizing 'Islamophobia'

A merica is a seething hotbed of "Islamophobia," filled with ignorant racist rubes who irrationally fear the benign Muslim religion, former Ambassador Thomas R. Pickering said in more polished, diplomatic language during a 2013 panel discussion at the National Cathedral in Washington, D.C.

The official topic for the evening was "what role the faith community can play in fighting Islamophobia," a make-believe mental illness that Islamic militants would love to have listed in the psychiatrist's *vade mecum*, the *Diagnostic and Statistical Manual of Mental Disorders* (a.k.a. the DSM).

In a particularly revealing soliloquy, Arab American Institute president James J. Zogby, whose younger brother is renowned pollster John Zogby, passionately inveighed against his fellow Americans.

Zogby, who is also managing director of Zogby Research Services., saved special scorn for Tea Party movement supporters, labeling them dangerous racist Islamophobes:

> **I think that there's a direct correlation between the president of the United States and Islamophobia. As we do our polling, we find that it is not the universal phenomenon. This hatred toward Muslims is largely concentrated with middle class, middle age, white people, and then it overlaps almost identically with the Tea Party. It is not a Republican thing. It's a generational thing.**

Zogby trots out the typical tropes leftists used to explain benighted conservatives. They're disenchanted haters, unemployed losers, and disillusioned people who constantly get the short end of the stick.

> **And it is a phenomenon born of a simple set of conditions, collapse of home mortgages, foreclosures increasing, pensions in collapse when the stock market went down, unemployment doubling, the decline of the American dream. In our polling we always used, when we'd say, are your children going to be better off than you, that's the American dream question, we'd get two thirds saying yes. We now get two thirds saying no.**

And in the midst of all of that this group of white middle aged, middle class men looked around and saw a young African-American, educated at Harvard with a middle name Hussein, and didn't like the president of the United States of America. It fueled this phenomenon and it opened the door for the wedge issue to operate and it's operating simply among that demographic. It's not a universal phenomenon. It's not found among African-Americans or Asians or Latinos. It's not found among young white kids. It's not found among college educated professional women. It's found in that one narrow demographic. That's where the bad numbers come from.

He continued: "I have a lot of gripes with George Bush, but if he were president, he would be doing what he did, which is put his foot down and say stop. I think we would not be seeing the phenomenon growing as we see it growing. But the problem is that if Barack Obama says stop, they say you're just the damn problem to begin with, you're not one of us anyway," Zogby said.

There is "an overlay between the racism and the Islamophobia" that is "being used as a wedge issue" against President Obama, he said. Zogby, whom Obama appointed to the U.S. Commission on International Religious Freedom, also described controversial U.S. Rep. Keith Ellison (D-Minn.), a Muslim left-winger with close ties to the Muslim Brotherhood who co-chairs the Congressional Progressive Caucus, as "a gift to America and Congress, an extraordinary person who could not be better than he is."

It should be noted that Zogby's views are unremarkable in leftist circles. They are within the mainstream of the Democratic Party. In fact he is a Democratic National Committee official. In 1984, Zogby was a senior advisor to the Rev. Jesse Jackson's presidential campaign.[71]

Spawning Hoaxes

The Left knows there is no better way to spread the word about a cause than to have a good story. If there is no story, the Left makes one up. Manufacturing victims is a good way to win support for the phony anti-Islamophobia cause. The mainstream media helps out by taking incidents involving Muslims and assuming before the evidence is in that the persons were targeted because of their faith. When assailants are Muslim, the media

---

[71] "Lifting the veil on the 'Islamophobia' hoax," by Matthew Vadum, *Foundation Watch*, December 2015, https://capitalresearch.org/2015/11/islamophobia-hoax/, accessed June 11, 2016

often push the storyline that they were mentally ill and not motivated to act because of their adherence to Islam.

SAADIQ LONG, the American-born Muslim convert promoted by the Left as a victim of Islamophobia was arrested in late 2015 in Turkey near the Syrian border, accused of being part of an Islamic State terror cell. Long became a media darling after he was placed on the U.S. government's no-fly list, which prevented him from flying from his current home in Qatar to his native Oklahoma to see his ailing mother. In 2013 the HAMAS offshoot, Council on American-Islamic Relations (CAIR), protested on Long's behalf, claiming he was a "Muslim man sentenced to life without air travel." Marxist muckraker Glenn Greenwald howled that Long was "effectively exiled from his own country," and leftist Kevin Drum of *Mother Jones* lamented that Long was trapped in the "Kafkaesque World of the No-Fly List." Eventually the government caved in and allowed Long to fly to the U.S. While stateside, police returned him to the list, preventing his return to Qatar. He hopped on a bus and flew out of Mexico and was later picked up by Turkish authorities along with other accused terrorists.

AHMED MOHAMED, the 14-year-old student who was briefly detained and suspended from MacArthur High School in Irving, Texas, in September 2015 for bringing a disassembled clock that resembled an IED timing device to class, threatened to sue the school district and city for $15 million in damages. Soon after, the international poster child for so-called Islamophobia moved to the Islamic-supremacist state of Qatar. WND has reported on various school disciplinary actions, including "weeks of suspensions" handed out to the unruly student. Ralph Kubiak, a former history teacher of Ahmed's, described him as a "weird little kid" who built a remote control to interfere with a classroom projector. He said Ahmed was the kind of child who "could either be CEO of a company or head of a gang." Following the incident, Ahmed was feted at the White House by President Barack Obama. Before meeting the president, he said, "I'm going to talk to [Obama] about, like, how hard it is growing up in America. It was pretty hard living in America and going to school being Muslim." Obama previously tweeted in support of Ahmed, praising his so-called clock, and inviting him for a visit: "Cool clock, Ahmed. Want to bring it to the White House? We should inspire more kids like you to like science. It's what makes America great." CAIR took up the teenager's cause with gusto, arranging a publicity blitzkrieg to hype his case. CAIR honored him with its "American Muslim of the Year" award.[72]

---

[72] In early January 2017, a Texas judge dismissed the defamation lawsuit filed in September 2016 by Ahmed's father against Glenn Beck and the Center for Security Policy. A separate lawsuit remains pending against the Irving, TX, school district.

TAHERA AHMAD, an Associate Muslim chaplain at Northwestern University who openly posts her Muslim Brotherhood links at the school website,[73] claimed to have been denied an unopened Diet Coke on a United Airlines flight during the summer of 2016. The flight attendant insisted on opening the soda first, which was unacceptable to Ahmad, who promptly complained about Islamophobia and received an ocean of media coverage. As Daniel Greenfield of the David Horowitz Freedom Center quipped, "On a scale of hate crimes this is somewhere between 0 and -0.02. About the only person who could possibly complain about it is a celebrity whose color allotment of M&Ms is specified in a rider to their contract or a professional Islamic grievance-monger looking for any excuse to play victim." Some activists actually likened Ahmad to Rosa Parks. "The TSA isn't too fond of passengers having closed cans of soda on them," adds Greenfield. "It may have something to do with when a Muslim woman attempted to bring down a China Southern Airlines flight to Beijing using soda cans that she had injected with flammable liquid and dropped in the bathroom trash can." CAIR's Chicago branch took up the case, demanding in June 2015 that United Airlines publicly apologize, acknowledge "egregious" discrimination occurred, and force its staff to undergo "sensitivity training."[74]

IBRAHIM ABU MOHAMMED, the Grand Mufti of Australia blamed Islamophobia, as opposed to Islamic terrorists, for the coordinated mass-casualty terrorist attacks in Paris, France in November 2015 and the media helped him get his message out. "It is therefore imperative that all causative factors such as racism, Islamophobia … duplicitous foreign policies and military intervention must be comprehensively addressed," he said. "In addition any discourse which attempts to apportion blame by association or sensationalizes violence to stigmatize a certain segment of society only serves to undermine community harmony and safety," he said in the wake of the slaughter of 130 innocent people. The *Daily Mail* reported July 16, 2016, that investigators told an official inquiry that the victims killed at the Bataclan nightclub had their eyes gouged out, genitals cut off and stuffed in their mouths, and that women were stabbed in their genitals. Police attending to the scene reportedly vomited when they found the bodies. Islamic State was said to have captured

---

http://dailycaller.com/2017/01/10/texas-judge-dismisses-clock-boys-defamation-lawsuit-against-conservatives/

[73] See Tahera Ahmed's profile here: http://www.northwestern.edu/millarchapel/about-us/meet-the-staff/tahera-ahmad/

[74] Tahera Ahmed later made headlines again when, during 20 January 2017 protests in Chicago against the inauguration of President Donald Trump, she closed the program over loud speakers with the *adhan,* or Islamic call to prayer. http://www.centerforsecuritypolicy.org/2017/01/25/red-green-axis-takes-to-the-streets-of-chicago/

the torture sessions on video and was planning to use them in propaganda videos.

These hoaxes are not isolated incidents. This is not an exhaustive list.[75]

Foundations and nonprofits on the anti-Islamophobia bandwagon

The idea that there is such a thing as Islamophobia aids America's enemies and is promoted by activists and others. Abdur-Rahman Muhammad, a former member of the Herndon, Va.-based International Institute for Islamic Thought (IIIT), now rejects the idea of Islamophobia. "This loathsome term is nothing more than a thought-terminating cliché conceived in the bowels of Muslim think tanks for the purpose of beating down critics."

But the left-wing philanthropic establishment maintains that Islamophobia is an evil related to discrimination and xenophobia.

According to George Soros's Open Society Foundations (formerly Open Society Institute), Islamophobia is a term that is wielded by the righteous:

... alongside structural discrimination affecting Muslims, in order to counter the discriminatory effects of an ideology of cultural superiority similar to racism in which attitudes, behaviors, and policies reject, exclude, vilify, or deny equal treatment to Muslims. Such discrimination is based on real or perceived Muslim background; or racial, ethnic and national origins which are associated with this background.

OSF gives grants aimed at countering Islamophobia and sponsors panel discussions such as "The Cultural War on Terror: Race, Policy, and Propaganda," which took place in 2015 in New York City and was moderated by left-wing journalist Peter Beinart.

Right after 9/11, the far-left George Soros-funded Tides Foundation created a "9/11 Fund" to advocate a "peaceful national response" to the Islamic terrorist attacks. Tides later received an OSF grant and renamed the fund the Democratic Justice Fund. Tides founder Drummond Pike, who played a major role in covering up a million-dollar embezzlement at the former Association of Community Organizations for Reform Now (ACORN), sat on the board of the Environmental Working Group alongside Fenton Communications founder David Fenton. Fenton's leftist public relations firm created "an ad campaign for the liberal media group Fairness and Accuracy

---

[75] "Lifting the veil on the 'Islamophobia' hoax," by Matthew Vadum, *Foundation Watch*, December 2015, https://capitalresearch.org/2015/11/islamophobia-hoax/, accessed June 11, 2016

in Reporting that falsely depicted" broadcaster Bill O'Reilly "as a bigot, liar and 'Islamophobe.'"[76]

The 2008 PR campaign promoted by FAIR was called, "Smearcasting: How Islamophobes Spread Bigotry, Fear and Misinformation." The list included what FAIR described as "some of the media's leading teachers of anti-Muslim bigotry, serving various roles in the Islamophobic movement." Apart from O'Reilly, those targeted were: authors Michelle Malkin, Mark Steyn, David Horowitz, and Robert Spencer; broadcasters Glenn Beck, Sean Hannity, and Michael Savage; Investigative Project on Terrorism founder Steven Emerson; and Christian evangelist Pat Robertson.

The Chicago-based Joyce Foundation funds Muslim outreach campaigns. A 2012 program was called "Uniting Christianity, Islam, and Judaism Through Dance." Barack Obama sat on the foundation's board from 1994 to 2002.

Foundation grants find their way to nonprofits that aim to silence critics of Islam by painting them as bigoted and ignorant, unaware of the "real" peaceful religion founded by Muhammad.

Major foundation-funded nonprofit sources of anti-Islamophobia propaganda in the United States include: Brennan Center for Justice at New York University School of Law (BCJ); Council on American-Islamic Relations (CAIR); Center for American Progress (CAP); Institute for Policy Studies (IPS); Media Matters for America (MMfA); and Southern Poverty Law Center (SPLC).

Here, according to IRS filings, are the foundations funding those six groups:

- Annie E. Casey Foundation, Baltimore, Md. (has funded BCJ with $280,000 since 2002, CAP and CAP Action $1.28 million since 2008, IPS $65,000 since 2005, SPLC $179,000 since 2008);

- Arca Foundation, Washington, D.C. (BCJ $125,000 since 2001, IPS $689,200 since 2001, MMfA $150,000 since 2004);

- Bauman Family Foundation, Washington, D.C. (BCJ $1,482,500 since 2006, MMfA since $450,000 since 2005);

- Bohemian Foundation, Fort Collins, Colo. (BCJ $300,000 since 2009, MMfA $2.37 million since 2005);

- Carnegie Corp. of New York, New York, N.Y. (CAP $4.5 million since 2009, MMfA $50,000 since 2008);

- Nathan Cummings Foundation, New York, N.Y. (CAP $1.93 million since 2005, IPS $120,000 since 1999);

---

[76] "The Great Smear Machine," by Rowan Scarborough, Human Events, April 10, 2009

- Ford Foundation, New York, N.Y. (CAP $9.69 million since 2009, IPS $1.91 million since 1999, MMfA $3.24 million since 2010);
- Foundation to Promote Open Society, New York, N.Y. (CAP $5.7 million since 2010, IPS $725,000 since 2009, MMfA $1.27 million since 2010);
- Gill Foundation, Denver, Colo. (CAP $995,000 since 2006, MMfA $1,730,000 since 2006, SPLC $25,000 since 2005);
- Glaser Progress Foundation, Seattle, Wash. (CAP $2.166 million since 2003, MMfA $801,000 since 2005);
- Joyce Foundation, Chicago, Ill. (BCJ $1 million since 1998, CAP $1.51 million since 2005, MMfA $400,000 since 2010);
- John D. & Catherine T. MacArthur Foundation, Chicago, Ill. (CAP $229,575 since 2006, IPS $820,900 since 1999);
- Marisla Foundation, Laguna Beach, Calif. (CAP $8 million since 2004, MMfA $1.34 million since 2007);
- Charles Stewart Mott Foundation, Flint, Mich. (BCJ $105,000 since 2005, CAP $70,000 since 2007, IPS $2.58 million since 1999);
- Open Society Institute (a.k.a. Open Society Foundations), New York, N.Y. (CAP $4.35 million since 2005, IPS $75,000 since 2002);
- Public Welfare Foundation, Washington, D.C. (BCJ $510,000 since 2000, IPS $150,000 since 2007, SPLC $1,050,000 since 2008);
- Rockefeller Family Fund Inc., New York, N.Y. (BCJ $231,000 since 2004, CAP $202,500 since 2003);
- Rockefeller Foundation, New York, N.Y. (CAP $6.32 million since 2009, IPS $100,015 since 2003);
- Rockefeller Philanthropy Advisors, New York, N.Y. (CAIR $30,000 since 2008, SPLC $559,000 since 2002);
- Sandler Foundation, San Francisco, Calif. (CAP $42.7 million since 2004, MMfA $400,000 since 2005);
- Schumann Center for Media and Democracy, New York, N.Y. (BCJ $250,000 since 1999, IPS $233,060 since 1998, MMfA $600,000 since 2005);
- Stephen M. Silberstein Foundation, Belvedere, Calif. (BCJ $173,080 since 2008, CAP $2.95 million since 2003, MMfA $2.92 million since 2003);

- Silicon Valley Community Foundation, Mountain View, Calif. (CAIR $90,000 since 2008, CAP $190,000 since 2007, MMfA $1.11 million since 2008, SPLC $60,000 since 2005);

- Surdna Foundation, New York, N.Y. (BCJ $180,000 since 2005);

- Tides Foundation, San Francisco, Calif. (BCJ $2.98 million since 2002, CAIR $5,000 since 2002, IPS $1.25 million since 2002, MMfA $3.79 million since 2004, SPLC $103,000 since 2000); and

- Wallace Global Fund II, Washington, D.C. (BCJ $255,000 since 2010, CAP $150,000 since 2011, IPS $440,000 since 2009, MMfA $350,000 since 2009).

Just as the Left spread defeatism during the Cold War, its activists these days try to undermine Americans' will to fight sharia infiltration and resist domestic Islamization.

The Institute for Policy Studies (IPS) is a relic of the Cold War. But not on the American side. As Discover the Networks reports:

> **Throughout its history, the IPS has committed itself to the task of advancing leftist causes, working with agents of the Castro regime, championing environmentalist and anti-war positions in the 1960s and 1970s; declaring against the Reagan administration's efforts to roll back communism in the 1980s; joining the vanguard of what the IPS hails as the "anti-corporate globalization movement" in the 1990s; and, most recently, furnishing policy research assailing the 2003 U.S.-led war in Iraq.**

> **Begun in Washington, DC, IPS headquarters quickly became a resource center for national reporters and a place for KGB agents from the nearby Soviet embassy to convene and strategize. Cora Weiss headed one of the IPS's most successful forays – into Riverside Church in Manhattan. She was invited there in 1978 by the Reverend William Sloane Coffin to run the church's Disarmament Program, which sought to consolidate Soviet nuclear superiority in Europe – in the name of "peace." In 1982 Weiss helped organize the largest disarmament rally ever held. Staged in New York City, the rally was a coalition of communist organizations.[77]**

---

[77] "Institute for Policy Studies: History and Agendas," Discover the Networks, 2005, http://www.discoverthenetworks.org/Articles/ipshistoryandagenda.html, June 1, 2016

IPS, which describes itself on its website as "a community of public scholars and organizers linking peace, justice, and the environment in the U.S. and globally," regularly publishes anti-American, anti-Israeli, and Islamic propaganda on its website. IPS operates Right Web (rightweb.irc-online.org), a website whose tagline is "Tracking militarists' efforts to influence U.S. foreign policy." Phyllis Bennis, who directs the New Internationalism Project at IPS, pushes the oft-refuted line that poverty, the existence of Israel, and social ills drive people to commit acts of Islamic terrorism. Bombing Islamic State-held territory only makes things worse, she said, adding that the so-called root causes of instability in the region needs to be addressed. "As long as we're focusing solely on the military side and ignoring the conditions that lead people to turn to ISIS as a lesser evil, we're not going to be able to end these kinds of attacks" by Islamic State against civilians," she said.[78]

Media Matters for America, a manic "conservative misinformation" watchdog and character assassination shop funded by George Soros and run by discredited former journalist David Brock, spews left-wing propaganda and provides facile talking points for journalists to incorporate in their articles. In other words, MMfA hounds reporters, trying to push them leftward, while offering to do their thinking for them. The nonprofit group, which Hillary Clinton claims to have founded, pushes the Left's line on Islam every chance it gets. Sometimes the online content consists of little more than transcribing TV and radio programs.

After Muslim American immigration lawyer Khizr Khan chastised then-GOP standard-bearer, now President Donald Trump during the 2016 Democratic National Convention for his proposal to temporarily pause Muslim immigration to the U.S. as a means of combating terrorism, MMfA attacked the candidate over and over again trying to paint him as a bigot, racist, and Islamophobe. The group wheeled out the BBC's Kim Ghattas to trash Trump and Americans in general. Video from CNN showed Ghattas saying:

The other point is, what I've found very troubling with the Khan episode is that, every time the family's name comes up, Mr. Trump and his surrogates bring up Islamic terrorism. And the insinuation that somehow, whenever you speak about Muslim-Americans, you must bring up terrorism is very disturbing, and it feeds a pattern of Islamophobia. What Mr. Trump said about Ghazala Khan, that she stood there as a subdued wife and probably wasn't allowed to speak. Well, she

---

[78] "Our military approach to ISIS will only lead to more civilian casualties," by Phyllis Bennis, Institute for Policy Studies, July 6, 2016, http://www.ips-dc.org/military-approach-isis-will-lead-civilian-casualties/, July 15, 2016

showed him that she could speak, but the insinuation that Muslim women are downtrodden, that all Arab women are downtrodden is that Trump's probably never met one because I can tell you, they're pretty feisty.[79]

It seems never to have occurred to Ghattas that Khan, whose U.S. hero soldier son was killed in action in Iraq, was attacking Trump over his proposed Muslim immigration pause. Most fair-minded people would agree that when someone is verbally attacked he is entitled to defend himself. Nor did Ghattas consider the possibility that Khan was using his deceased son as a kind of human shield to deflect criticism. Khan, as those who watched the convention in Philadelphia know, implied that everyone who supports the Trump pause is a bigot. But left-wing reporters often can't grasp this kind of nuance and so it's easier to attack the figure they dislike.

Khizr and Ghazala Khan put their Muslim Brotherhood affiliations on public display when they showed up a few weeks later at the Islamic Society of North America (ISNA) annual conference in a Chicago suburb alongside senior Muslim Brotherhood leadership figures like Tariq Ramadan. At the gathering, ISNA President Azhar Azeez thanked the Khans for their "supreme sacrifices." Secretary of the Department of Homeland Security Jeh Johnson told the Brotherhood audience that his agency was "aligned" with their interests and that the story of Muslim Americans was "the quintessential American story." ISNA gave the Khans its Outstanding Ambassadors of Islam Award.[80]

Media Matters also smeared activist Brigitte Gabriel, a Lebanese-born Christian, calling her a "hate group" leader. Gabriel is a hater the Left claims, because, among other things, she said in a Fox News Channel appearance that Islamic Law is not compatible with the U.S. Constitution.

It's not compatible with our Constitution. They believe apostates should be killed. They believe a woman's value is half of that of a man. They believe if a woman is raped, she needs four witnesses in order for her to be saved, to testify against the rape. They believe in supremacy, they believe Islam is supreme to all other religions. They do not believe in

---

[79] "BBC's Kim Ghattas: Trump's Insinuations About American Muslims "Feeds A Pattern Of Islamophobia," Media Matters for America, Aug. 1, 2016, http://mediamatters.org/video/2016/08/01/bbc-s-kim-ghattas-trumps-insinuations-about-american-muslims-feeds-pattern-islamophobia/212058, accessed Aug. 2, 2016

[80] "Khans thank Islamic convention attendees, warn 'assault' on community will outlast election," by Grace Wong, *Chicago Tribune*, Sept. 3, 2016, http://www.chicagotribune.com/news/local/breaking/ct-khans-trump-speech-islamic-society--20160903-story.html, accessed Sept. 16, 2016

man-made laws such as the Constitution. That's just the tip of the iceberg, and that's why Sharia law is not compatible with the United States Constitution.[81]

When a woman like Gabriel speaks truth to power, the Left can be counted on to make an example of her.

The Ford Foundation both funds anti-Islamophobia campaigns and conducts its own.

The far-left philanthropy not only funds groups pushing the myth of Islamophobia but also provides platforms for radicals to denounce America and boost its Islamic supremacist enemies. A forum in early 2016 examined the "global threats and domestic political rhetoric [that] are fueling misguided fear, discrimination, and violence against American Muslims, Arabs, and South Asians." The New York region's "response to this crisis will be a bellwether for the rest of the country."

During a panel discussion, Fahd Ahmed, executive director of DRUM – South Asian Organizing Center, said America is hopelessly biased against Muslims and discrimination is everywhere. "The compartmentalization between social anti-Muslim bigotry and institutionalized and official forms of anti-Muslim policies, domestically and internationally, that distinction doesn't exist and so people see a very direct and organic relationship between them, even people who are not Muslims." Government policies, Ahmed said, make it acceptable to be an anti-Muslim bigot.

"I think why a lot of the social bigotry has become acceptable is over a decade worth of policies which officially sanction the marginalization of communities and say it is okay to be bigoted towards them. It's the government policies themselves [that] are affirming that."[82]

Ahmed's group DRUM, incidentally, doesn't appear to be particularly focused on Muslim advocacy; it is a garden variety ethnic left-wing community organizing group throwing its lot in with its left-wing allies. Its mission statement describes DRUM as "a multigenerational, membership led organization of low-wage South Asian immigrant workers and youth in New York City" that was founded in 2000. Its membership "is multigenerational and represents the diaspora of the South Asian community – Afghanistan,

---

[81] "Hate Group Leader Brigitte Gabriel Says The Faith of '1.6 Billion Muslims ... Is Not Compatible With Our Constitution,'" Media Matters for America, July 15, 2016, http://mediamatters.org/video/2016/07/15/hate-group-leader-brigitte-gabriel-says-faith-16-billion-muslims-not-compatible-our-constitution/211616, accessed Aug. 2, 2016

[82] "Confronting Islamophobia in America Today," Ford Foundation website, date unknown, https://www.fordfoundation.org/the-latest/ford-live-events/confronting-islamophobia-in-america-today/, accessed May 13, 2016. The forum was held in New York City on Feb. 2, 2016.

51

Bangladesh, Bhutan, Guyana, India, Nepal, Pakistan, Sri Lanka, and Trinidad."[83]

Then there is the much-investigated Bill, Hillary and Chelsea Clinton Foundation, which has disturbing ties to the world of Islamic terrorism. It isn't a "foundation" in the traditional sense of the term. It is a tax-exempt public charity that takes in donations. It is not primarily a grant-making organization which is generally speaking what a foundation is.

Americans ought to be concerned that the Clinton Foundation has raked in up to $57 million from sharia-adherent Muslim nations known for the barbaric treatment of those involved in same-sex relationships. Would Mrs. Clinton have felt somehow obligated to these governments had she become president in January 2017? Maybe she's fine with the repressive anti-gay policies of Muslim nations that enforce Islamic Law. News of the rivers of Muslim cash flowing into the foundation belie Clinton's claim to be a champion of gay rights.

The Muslim governments that hew to sharia doctrine on gays certainly can't complain. According to the Clinton Foundation's own disclosures, which give only ranges for gifts, donors include Algeria ($250,001 to $500,000); Kuwait ($5 million to $10 million); Morocco through its phosphate monopoly OCP (at least $1 million); Oman ($1 million to $5 million); Qatar, including its soccer agency ($1,250,001 to $5.5 million); and the United Arab Emirates ($1 million to $5 million). These countries penalize homosexual acts with prison, but the Clinton Foundation has also received donations from Brunei ($1 million to $5 million) and Saudi Arabia ($10 million to $25 million), both of which put homosexuals to death.

When Fox News Channel reporter William La Jeunesse reached out to left-of-center gay rights organizations about the blood money, they refused to criticize Clinton. Well, to be more precise, "more than a half-dozen prominent gay rights organizations including the Human Rights Campaign; GLAAD; the International Gay and Lesbian Human Rights Commission; the Los Angeles LGBT Center; and the Gill Foundation," failed to respond.[84]

Perhaps Clinton's ties to Islam prevent her from coming clean and returning those suspect donations. The Clinton Foundation had a Muslim Brotherhood-connected operative on its payroll for five years. Gehad el-Haddad was a spokesman for the Clinton Climate Initiative who quit and later became a Muslim Brotherhood spokesman. In 2015, Haddad received a life

---

[83] "About Us," DRUM – South Asian Organizing Center website, date unknown, http://www.drumnyc.org/about-us/, accessed May 13, 2016. DRUM stands for "Desis Rising Up and Moving."

[84] "Rights groups silent as Clinton Foundation takes millions from countries that imprison gays," by William La Jeunesse, Fox News, June 17, 2016, http://www.foxnews.com/politics/2016/06/17/rights-groups-silent-as-clinton-foundation-takes-millions-from-countries-that-imprison-gays.html, accessed June 17, 2016

sentence in Egypt for sedition. And longtime lieutenant Huma Abedin, later vice-chairman of Clinton's 2016 presidential campaign, worked for the Clinton Foundation but has deep generational and personal connections to the Muslim Brotherhood as well as Saudi al-Qa'eda financier Abdullah Omar Nasseef. We can only wonder what advice Abedin, who also worked for Clinton at the State Department, gave Secretary Clinton. Would the disastrous Islamic Uprising of 2011 or the U.S.-NATO invasion of Libya have happened without Abedin's influence over governmental decision-making processes? We may never know.[85]

Focus on the Brennan Center for Justice

The Brennan Center for Justice at New York University treats Islamic supremacism as much ado about nothing.

One Brennan Center paper by Faiza Patel argues in all seriousness that there is little point in searching for terrorists within the Muslim community because the connection between Muslim terrorism and Islam is shaky at best. Patel oversells a dubious British study that she claims "explicitly debunked" the connection between religiosity and terrorism.

"Far from being religious zealots, a large number of those involved in terrorism do not practise their faith regularly," the study states. "Many lack religious literacy and could actually be regarded as religious novices."[86]

This is, of course, an absurd argument. It may be true that not all Muslim terrorists pray five times a day and observe all the Islamic commandments. This may have something to do with the Islamic doctrine on dying a *shaheed* while waging jihad against infidels that holds their sins are washed away, clearing the way for them to be welcomed into paradise in the afterlife.

It was widely reported that in the lead-up to 9/11 that Mohamed Atta, the ultra-devout ringleader of the attacks who crashed the first hijacked airliner into the World Trade Center, and his co-conspirators spent a lot of time drinking in strip bars and doing things like receiving lap dances that may have gotten them flogged in observant Islamic countries.[87]

---

[85] "Hillary Clinton's LGBT hypocrisy," by Matthew Vadum, Daily Caller, July 6, 2016, http://dailycaller.com/2016/07/06/hillary-clintons-lgbt-hypocrisy/

[86] "Rethinking Radicalization," by Faiza Patel, Brennan Center website, 2011, p.10, https://www.brennancenter.org/sites/default/files/legacy/RethinkingRadicalization.pdf, accessed May 9, 2016

[87] "Seedy Secrets of Hijackers Who Broke Muslims' Laws, by Toby Harnden, Telegraph, Oct. 6, 2001, http://www.telegraph.co.uk/news/1358665/Seedy-secrets-of-hijackers-who-broke-Muslim-laws.html, accessed May 9, 2016

Osama bin Laden gave the jihadis a free pass. He acknowledged that even though "those youth who conducted operations did not accept any *fiqh* [Islamic laws]" they nonetheless adhered to the legal principles of Islam.[88]

Ignoring the violence-laden content of the Qur'an, Patel even makes the argument that faithful Muslims learned in the ways of Islam are *less* likely to embrace terrorism. She insists studies show that "[i]nstead of promoting radicalization, a strong religious identity could well serve to inoculate people against turning to violence in the name of Islam."[89]

At "Countering Violent Extremism: A Briefing," a Brennan Center conference in 2015, scholars and activists expressed dismay even at the Obama administration's half-hearted efforts to combat what it calls "violent extremism." Arun Kundnani, a London-born former Open Society fellow who teaches at NYU, complained about the strictures that government research grants place on academic freedom. He also said government efforts to combat terrorism constitute attacks on Muslims. "The bulk of the funding has been to fund people who are saying things that the government wants to hear, saying things that will be serviceable to a preexisting law enforcement agenda which is about essentially criminalizing a community."[90]

Kundnani is also the author of a book with the mocking title of *The Muslims Are Coming!: Islamophobia, Extremism, and the Domestic War on Terror*, that was published in 2014 by Verso. MSNBC describes the publishing house as "the radical left-wing Verso Books."[91]

At the website of Qatar-based Al Jazeera, Kundnani bashes Americans for their views on Islam. "Since the 1970s, Muslims have repeatedly been stereotyped in the US as dangerous terrorists. But, over the last six years, a new fear of Muslims has gradually entered the conservative mainstream: that

---

[88] "Al-Nass al-kamil li sharit al-fidiyu al-mansub li Bin Ladin," at http://www.uaegoal.com/vb/showthread.php?t=924, accessed Feb 8, 2008, as cited in Engaging the Muslim World, by Juan Cole, Palgrave MacMillan, 2009, p. 77. Presumably Cole translated the source document which is written in Arabic.

[89] "Rethinking Radicalization," by Faiza Patel, Brennan Center for Justice, 2011, p.10, https://www.brennancenter.org/sites/default/files/legacy/RethinkingRadicalization.pdf, accessed May 9, 2016

[90] "Lifting the Veil on the 'Islamophobia' Hoax," by Matthew Vadum, Foundation Watch, December 2015, https://capitalresearch.org/2015/11/islamophobia-hoax/. The conference, "Countering Violent Extremism: A Briefing," sponsored by the Brennan Center and the Campaign for Liberty, took place Oct. 30, 2015 at the National Press Club in Washington, D.C.

[91] "The 25 best things we learned from Bernie Sanders' book," by Alex Seitz-Wald, MSNBC website, May 28, 2015, http://www.msnbc.com/msnbc/the-25-best-things-we-learned-bernie-sanders-book, accessed May 21, 2016

Muslims are taking over the United States and imposing 'sharia law.'" These fears "are paranoid and lack any basis in reality," he adds.[92]

American Muslims face the same kind of persecution Jews faced a century ago, Kundnani improbably claims. Cueing the violins, he writes

A century ago, America's Jews were likewise seen as infiltrators threatening Western values. Central to US anti-Semitic ideology was also a conspiracy theory that presented Jews as secretly pulling the strings of international finance and world revolution. ... The modern discourse over Muslims today resembles the manner in which Jews were talked about then. In both cases, a religious minority is seen as a dangerous underclass destroying society from below with their alien values, as well as a hidden force secretly controlling the world from above, through their infiltration of centres of power. American Jews were eventually able to overcome the worst anti-Semitism of the 20th century and establish security and equality in the US. Will Muslims be able to do the same?[93]

Kundnani, unlike most left-wing Islamic sympathizers, makes little effort to conceal his contempt for America. He admits that campaigning against Islamophobia advances leftism. Fighting "anti-Muslim conspiracy theories and all of their accompanying rhetoric are not just about defending the civil rights of Muslims in the US. It is also about removing one of the ideological supports of US imperialism."[94]

Kundnani also thinks Americans need to lighten up and stop worrying about whether Muslims really mean what they say. "I think we need to abandon the language of radicalization and extremism and focus much more narrowly on the question of acts of violence specifically," he said at the Brennan Center event. "In this country we nowadays have a situation where

---

[92] "The belief system of the Islamophobes," by Arun Kundnani, Al Jazeera website, Oct. 9, 2015, http://www.aljazeera.com/indepth/opinion/2015/10/belief-system-islamophobes-151006080105432.html, accessed May 21, 2016

[93] "The belief system of the Islamophobes," by Arun Kundnani, Al Jazeera website, Oct. 9, 2015, http://www.aljazeera.com/indepth/opinion/2015/10/belief-system-islamophobes-151006080105432.html, accessed May 21, 2016

[94] "The belief system of the Islamophobes," by Arun Kundnani, Al Jazeera website, Oct. 9, 2015, http://www.aljazeera.com/indepth/opinion/2015/10/belief-system-islamophobes-151006080105432.html, accessed May 21, 2016

what would be called dissent when expressed by a Muslim, gets called extremism."[95]

The Brennan Center takes the position that Countering Violent Extremism, the anti-terrorism initiative the Obama administration launched in 2014, is generally ineffective and often harmful. Its CVE Resource Page advises that CVE programs are nothing new and that they have "focused only on Muslims, stigmatizing them as a suspect community. These programs have further promoted flawed theories of terrorist radicalization which leads to unnecessary fear, discrimination, and unjustified reporting to law enforcement."[96]

Focus on the Center for American Progress

The Center for American Progress, founded by John Podesta, a veteran of the Clinton and Obama White Houses, has devoted significant resources to combating the phantom the Left calls Islamophobia. CAP is working hard to convince Americans that this make-believe mental illness of Islamophobia is a threat to American democracy and pluralism. CAP claims a $57 million network "is fueling Islamophobia in the United States." Among other projects, CAP created a sophisticated, flashy website (Islamophobianetwork.com) that identifies leading alleged Islamophobes. The site draws upon "Fear, Inc.: The Roots of the Islamophobia Network in America," a 2011 CAP report, and "Fear, Inc. 2.0: The Islamophobia Network's Efforts to Manufacture Hate in America," a CAP report from 2015.

CAP warns that there is "a small, tightly networked group of misinformation experts guiding an effort that reaches millions of Americans through effective advocates, media partners, and grassroots organizing." These people, particularly six key individuals and their organizations, spread "hate and misinformation."[97]

The six the website targets for vilification are, in alphabetical order:

- Steven Emerson, founder and executive director of the Investigative Project on Terrorism (IPT)

---

[95] "Lifting the Veil on the 'Islamophobia' Hoax," by Matthew Vadum, *Foundation Watch*, December 2015, https://capitalresearch.org/2015/11/islamophobia-hoax/. The conference, "Countering Violent Extremism: A Briefing," sponsored by the Brennan Center and the Campaign for Liberty, took place Oct. 30, 2015 at the National Press Club in Washington, D.C.

[96] "Countering Violent Extremism (CVE) A Resource Page," last updated May 15, 2016, Brennan Center website, https://www.brennancenter.org/analysis/cve-programs-resource-page, accessed May 21, 2016

[97] "About the Project," Islamophobia Network website, date unknown, https://islamophobianetwork.com/about, accessed May 5, 2016

- Frank Gaffney, founder and president of the Center for Security Policy (CSP)
- David Horowitz, founder and CEO of the David Horowitz Freedom Center
- Daniel Pipes, founder and president of the Middle East Forum (MEF)
- Robert Spencer, co-founder of Stop Islamization of America, director of Jihad Watch, vice president of American Freedom Defense Initiative (AFDI)
- David Yerushalmi, founder of the Society of Americans for National Existence (SANE), and general counsel for the CSP and Stop Islamization of America

The CAP-run website tries to discredit the six men by stating or implying, often without offering any proof, that they are "radical right-wing," ignorant, misinformed, paranoid, or bigoted. It smears CSP's Gaffney, for example, claiming he "makes unsubstantiated claims," and publishes commissioned papers whose authors knowingly arrive at "exaggerated and incorrect conclusions."[98]

The website also attacks respected author and activist Ayaan Hirsi Ali, a Somali-born ex-Muslim who is a fierce critic of Islam. It notes disapprovingly that she calls Islam "a destructive, nihilistic cult of death" and says we will lose the fight against terrorism "unless we realize that it's not just with extremist elements within Islam, but the ideology of Islam itself."

Although CAP is critical of Hirsi Ali, others see her as heroic and courageous, in the face of death threats for her criticisms of female genital mutilation and other barbaric practices. Named one of the 100 most influential persons by *Time* in 2005, Hirsi Ali has been a fellow at the American Enterprise Institute in Washington, D.C. and at Harvard's Kennedy School.[99]

Focus on the Southern Poverty Law Center

The far-left Southern Poverty Law Center relentlessly promotes the Big Lie, wildly popular in the media, that conservative Americans are racists and the real threat to the nation rather than sharia-promoting Islamic supremacists.

---

[98] "Frank Gaffney," Islamophobia Network website, date unknown, https://islamophobianetwork.com/misinformation-expert/frank-gaffney, May 5, 2016

[99] "Lifting the Veil on the 'Islamophobia' Hoax," by Matthew Vadum, *Foundation Watch*, December 2015, https://capitalresearch.org/2015/11/islamophobia-hoax/

Its tainted research and wild accusations have found their way into Department of Homeland Security bulletins. The group claims the principal enemies of the American people are Republican presidential nominee Donald Trump, conservatives, and the Tea Party movement.

The nonprofit SPLC is a leftist attack machine that has an astounding one third of a billion dollars ($338 million) in assets, as well as investments in Bermuda and the Cayman Islands, two offshore tax havens. The Center characterizes all opposition to immigration and open borders as symptomatic of hate and all political expression of those views to be hate speech. Disagree with founder Morris Dees or his staffers and you are evil and worthy of public condemnation. It may take some intellectual toughness to insist that the nation has the right to decide who may or may not cross its borders, but it's not hate.

Following the jihad massacre at a gay club in Orlando in June 2016, the group has played an integral role in the Left's propaganda push aimed at taking the focus away from gay-hating Islam and finding creative ways to blame conservatives and Republicans for the slaughter. Two days after Orlando, as a sea of rainbow flags rivaling those that washed over Facebook and Twitter following the Supreme Court's pro-same sex marriage ruling in *Obergefell v. Hodges* swept over social media, David Dinielli, deputy legal director of SPLC's LGBT Rights Project, tossed out a red herring as he complained amidst an unprecedented national outpouring of grief that somehow politicians weren't doing enough to characterize the attack as an assault on the gay community.

Instead of blaming Muslim terrorist Omar Mateen for the attack, Dinielli blamed people like President Donald Trump and Sen. Ted Cruz (R-Texas). Many politicians were secretly delighted so many gays were killed, he implied. "[M]any who offered their 'thoughts and prayers' know exactly what they are doing. They are trading on political expediency. The demonization of gay, lesbian, and transgender Americans pays, politically."

But this "demonization" of the LGBT community that the Southern Poverty Law Center complains of is pure paranoid fantasy. Anyone who followed media coverage in the days following the June 12 incident knows that cable TV and other media were filled with wall-to-wall denunciations of Mateen by politicians who acknowledged the sexual orientation of the victims whether explicitly or implicitly. Even those not generally sympathetic to gay rights made it clear that murder, including the murder of people based on their sexual preference, was morally abhorrent.[100]

---

[100] "The worst smear site in America," by Matthew Vadum, FrontPageMag, June 29, 2016, http://www.frontpagemag.com/fpm/263332/worst-smear-site-america-matthew-vadum, accessed June 11, 2016

THE SPLC draws up proposed lesson plans for teachers from pre-school/Kindergarten to the 12th grade. Its Teaching Tolerance site (Tolęrance.org) whitewashes Islam, painting it as just another monotheistic religion, like Judaism and Christianity. One webpage states:

> "Islam totally prohibits terrorism—there is no text that endorses that," says Ameena Jandali of the Islamic Networks Group. "Killing an innocent person is considered to be the greatest crime after worshiping another god." Teachers could ask students to brainstorm about other groups that have also engaged in terrorism or violence in the name of a religion and how that behavior ran counter to their faiths' core beliefs.

The same document depicts Islam as ahead of its time because it supposedly promoted women's rights long before Western Civilization did.

> Historically, Islam promoted women's rights. For instance, the Qur'an grants women freedoms that they did not have before, such as the right to inherit property, conduct business and have access to knowledge. "Men and women have the same responsibility before God, the same accountability before God," says Jandali. "Arranged marriages are more of a cultural practice—and women do have the right to divorce." In many cases, the oppression many women face in Muslim countries is caused by cultural tradition, not Islamic law.[101]

The word *jihad*, according to Teaching Tolerance, is strongly nuanced and widely misunderstood in the Western world. Perhaps this explains why Adolf Hitler's autobiographical manifesto, *Mein Kampf* (*My Struggle* in English), is marketed as *My Jihad* in Muslim countries.

> "Jihad" literally means striving, or doing one's utmost. Within Islam, there are two basic theological understandings of the word: The "Greater Jihad" is the struggle against the lower self – the struggle to purify one's heart, do good, avoid evil and make oneself a better person. The "Lesser Jihad" is an outward struggle. Jihad constitutes a moral principle to struggle against any obstacle that stands in the way of the

---

[101] "Debunking Misconceptions about Muslims and Islam," Teaching Tolerance, date not stated, http://www.tolerance.org/supplement/debunking-misconceptions-about-muslims-and-islam, accessed June 11, 2016

good. Bearing, delivering and raising a child, for example, is an example of outward jihad, because of the many obstacles that must be overcome to deliver and raise the child successfully. Jihad may also involve fighting against oppressors and aggressors who commit injustice. It is not "holy war" in the way a crusade would be considered a holy war, and while Islam allows and even encourages proselytizing, it forbids forced conversion.

Even jihadis are misunderstood, according to the Southern Poverty Law Center.[102]

---

[102] "Misunderstood Terms and Practices," Teaching Tolerance, date not stated, http://www.tolerance.org/publication/misunderstood-terms-and-practices, accessed June 11, 2016

CHAPTER 6
CAIR, the Number-One Muslim 'Civil Rights' Organization

Tax-exempt so-called civil rights organizations focusing on Muslim Americans abound. The most influential and high-profile by far is the Council on American-Islamic Relations (CAIR), a Muslim Brotherhood front group, which is, in fact, the U.S. HAMAS representative. Books have been written about CAIR and its corrosive effects on civil society and public discourse.

CAIR was established in Philadelphia, PA, in 1993 by the top HAMAS officials in the U.S. HAMAS, of course, is the Palestinian branch of the Muslim Brotherhood.

As such, CAIR is an agent of hostile foreign powers, including those in the business of exporting sharia and terrorism to our shores. CAIR has been appropriately compared to the German American Bund, a U.S.-based organization created before World War II to promote a favorable view of America's eventual enemy, Nazi Germany. The Bund, like CAIR, was a fifth-column organization created with the assistance of unfriendly foreign powers.

CAIR was founded by Nihad Awad, Omar Ahmad, and Rafeeq Jaber. The three men, according to substantial federal evidence, and the group's own documents, had close links to the Islamic Association for Palestine, which was created by senior HAMAS operative Mousa Abu Marzook to serve as the public relations and recruitment arm of HAMAS in the U.S. CAIR opened an office in the nation's capital with a $5,000 grant from the Marzook-founded Holy Land Foundation for Relief and Development, a charity that President George W. Bush shuttered in 2001 for collecting money to support HAMAS. CAIR called the action "unjust" and "disturbing." In 2004, Marzook was indicted on racketeering charges related to his pro-HAMAS activities. Ahmad was named as an unindicted co-conspirator in the Holy Land Foundation trial.[103]

Ahmad is on record saying in 1998 that Islam should dominate not just the U.S. but all countries. "If you choose to live here ... you have a responsibility to deliver the message of Islam," he said. Ahmad was paraphrased saying, "Islam isn't in America to be equal to any other faiths, but to become dominant. The Qur'an should be the highest authority in America, and Islam the only accepted religion on earth." Ahmad also said,

---

[103] "Lifting the veil on the 'Islamophobia' hoax," by Matthew Vadum, *Foundation Watch*, December 2015, https://capitalresearch.org/2015/11/islamophobia-hoax/, accessed June 11, 2016

"Everything we need to know is in the Qur'an. We don't need to look somewhere else."

Sabotaging law enforcement and counter-terrorism programs is just part of CAIR's repertoire. CAIR has urged Muslims not to cooperate with the FBI, which it characterizes as corrupt. It applauded CIA director John Brennan and President Obama for following its recommendations by avoiding the word *Islamist* (a dubious term at best, but here opposed even when used by sympathizers). "Islamist is a stealth slur," the group says. "It exists as a piece of coded language."[104]

"Contending that American Muslims are the victims of wholesale repression, CAIR has provided sensitivity training to police departments across the United States, instructing law officers in the art of dealing with Muslims respectfully[,]" according to DiscoverTheNetworks. The estate of 9/11 victim John O'Neill Sr., a high-ranking FBI counter-terrorism agent, filed a lawsuit asserting that CAIR's goal "is to create as much self-doubt, hesitation, fear of name-calling, and litigation within police department and intelligence agencies as possible so as to render such authorities in effective in pursuing international and domestic terrorist entities."

CAIR and its allies have spent years lobbying the FBI to give Muslims special leeway in investigations. As of March 2012, FBI agents weren't allowed to treat individuals associated with terrorist groups automatically as potential threats to the nation, according to an FBI directive titled, "Guiding Principles: Touchstone Document on Training." The fact that a terrorism suspect is associated with a terrorist group is insufficient, according to the document, if that group also conducts other activities that are not terrorist in nature. It's a "don't ask, don't tell" policy that benefits terrorists.

FBI agents are instructed that "mere association with organizations that demonstrate both legitimate (advocacy) and illicit (violent extremism) objectives should not automatically result in a determination that the associated individual is acting in furtherance of the organization's illicit objective(s)," the document states. This is a bizarre kind of procedural fairness as viewed in a funhouse mirror, applying something akin to the criminal law "beyond a reasonable doubt" standard to an FBI investigation. Such an evidentiary threshold may be appropriate for a criminal trial, but it sets the bar far too high for mere investigations.[105]

---

[104] "CAIR's money laundering scheme," by Matthew Vadum, FrontPageMag, Sept. 23, 2013, http://www.frontpagemag.com/fpm/205183/cairs-money-laundering-scheme-matthew-vadum; it may be noted that neither "Islamism" nor "Islamist" exists in the Arabic language, but as used in the English language are made-up terms.

[105] "Lifting the veil on the 'Islamophobia' hoax," by Matthew Vadum, *Foundation Watch*, December 2015, https://capitalresearch.org/2015/11/islamophobia-hoax/, accessed June 11, 2016

CAIR's Extensive Political Connections

Since its creation, CAIR has posed as a civil rights organization in order to immunize itself from criticism. It has enjoyed remarkable success in infiltrating the American political establishment. Indeed, the Obama administration went out of its way to aid CAIR over and over again. The Obama administration has admitted to "hundreds" of closed-door meetings with CAIR.[106]

CAIR works tirelessly to undermine measures aimed at keeping jihadists out of the U.S. For example, in May 2016, it raised the alarm about legislation that would make it tougher for immigrants and visitors from terrorism-producing Muslim countries such as Iran, Iraq, Libya, Somalia, Syria, Sudan, and Yemen to get visas for the U.S. "This law would force a British national visa applicant born to a Syrian father who possess dual citizenship to undergo an intensive and lengthy background check usually reserved for suspected terrorists," CAIR Government Affairs Director Robert McCaw warned. "Once again, we see our government attempting to create a separate class of security screenings for Muslims traveling to America based on their religion and not on suspicion of any wrongdoing. This law will have an adverse impact on American Muslim families trying to connect with visiting relatives from overseas."[107]

CAIR has scores of left-wing federal lawmakers in its pocket.

U.S. Rep. John Conyers (D-Mich.), the former House Judiciary Committee chairman, has referred to CAIR's "long and distinguished history." He wants to kill the USA PATRIOT Act, stop the FBI from profiling Muslim suspects in terror investigations, and criminalize "disrespect" of Islam. At a 2007 CAIR banquet, U.S. Jim McDermott (D-Wash.) praised CAIR, saying "I always enjoy being with people like CAIR because you inspire me really to keep fighting … and I think that's why this kind of organization is so important for people to understand that you have a right to say whatever you believe. And I think you ought to exercise that. That's being a real American." U.S. Rep. Sheila Jackson-Lee (D-Texas) has spoken at many CAIR banquets. "How proud I am to have been associated with CAIR's legislative work in the

---

[106] "CAIR's money laundering scheme," by Matthew Vadum FrontPageMag, Sept. 23, 2013, http://www.frontpagemag.com/fpm/205183/cairs-money-laundering-scheme-matthew-vadum

[107] "CAIR Action Alert: Tell Congress to Stop Singling Out Travelers From Muslim Majority Countries," CAIR website, May 26, 2016, http://www.cair.com/government-affairs/legislative-action-center.html, accessed May 27, 2016. The bill in question, introduced in the 114th Congress by U.S. Rep. Randy Forbes (R-Va.), was H.R. 5203, the proposed "Visa Integrity and Security Act of 2016." On 27 January 2017, President Donald J. Trump issued an Executive Order, "Protecting the Nation from Foreign Terrorist Entry into the United States," which called for a temporary halt to refugee admission and entry from seven Muslim-majority countries. http://apps.washingtonpost.com/g/documents/national/read-the-executive-order-by-the-trump-administration-on-extreme-vetting/2310/

United States ... We need CAIR and we need all of you supporting CAIR," she said at one dinner in 2007. U.S. Rep. John Dingell (D-Mich.), who retired from Congress in 2015, said "my office door is always open" to CAIR.[108]

Even talking about Muslim terrorism is "really frightening" to her Muslim constituents, Rep. Jan Schakowsky (D-Ill.) complained in December 2015. Republican "words are terrorizing" Americans, said the longtime CAIR ally.[109]

CAIR allies in the U.S. House, House Minority Whip Steny Hoyer (D-Md.), Rep. Don Beyer (D-Va.), Del. Eleanor Holmes Norton (D-D.C.), Reps. Joe Crowley (D-N.Y.), Ellison and Carson, Mike Honda (D-Calif.), Betty McCollum (D-Minn.), and Schakowsky all denounced Republican presidential nominee Donald Trump's proposal to temporarily ban Muslim immigration. They put forward a proposed "Freedom of Religion Act" backed by CAIR that would keep Muslim immigrants flowing into the U.S. The measure would "prohibit the use of religious litmus tests as a means to ban immigrants, refugees, and international visitors trying to enter the United States." The lawmakers said the bill was introduced as a "response to political rhetoric vilifying select religious groups and increasingly hostile rhetoric toward religious freedom in the immigration system."[110]

"We cannot allow fear and paranoia to drive our public policy, especially when it comes to the defining values of our country," said Beyer. "Our Founding Fathers guaranteed religious freedom for all in the First Amendment to our Constitution. People all around the world look to us as the standard for freedom, liberty, and tolerance." Ellison attacked Trump, saying that when "presidential candidates talk about closing our borders to people of a certain faith, they aren't just being prejudiced – they're being un-American."[111]

Bill backer Schakowsky fell back on clichés. "As a nation of immigrants, we should welcome all who come to this country regardless of their religion or ethnic background," she said. "It is outrageous that many in this country are fanning the flames of hatred and intolerance by pushing for a religious test to enter the country." Carson added that "blocking immigrants because

---

[108] *Muslim Mafia: Inside the secret underworld that's conspiring to Islamize America*, by Paul David Gaubatz and Paul Sperry, WND Books, 2009, pp.193-4,198

[109] "Dem Rep Schakowsky: GOP Words 'Are Terrorizing' American Muslims," by Pam Key, Breitbart, Dec. 6, 2015, http://www.breitbart.com/video/2015/12/06/dem-rep-schakowsky-gop-words-are-terrorizing-american-muslims/, accessed May 3, 2016

[110] "House Delegation Introduces Religious Freedom Bill," website of Rep. Don Beyer, May 11, 2016, https://beyer.house.gov/news/documentsingle.aspx?DocumentID=341, accessed May 20, 2016

[111] "House Delegation Introduces Religious Freedom Bill," website of Rep. Don Beyer, May 11, 2016, https://beyer.house.gov/news/documentsingle.aspx?DocumentID=341, accessed May 20, 2016

of their religion would send a demoralizing and dangerous message to the world that the United States is no longer a beacon of freedom."[112]

The Left sticks together, whatever the issue. Not surprisingly CAIR's legislation was embraced by the usual suspects. Among the many left-of-center activist organizations endorsing it were: American Civil Liberties Union (ACLU); American Federation of State, County and Municipal Employees (AFSCME); Americans United for Separation of Church and State; Amnesty International USA; Anti-Defamation League; Emerge USA; Institute for Policy Studies; League of United Latin American Citizens (LULAC); National Center for Lesbian Rights; National Immigration Forum; People for the American Way; and the Southern Poverty Law Center.[113]

Ben Carson, CAIR, and the San Bernardino Massacre

Then-GOP presidential candidate Ben Carson took shots at CAIR in mid-December 2015. Carson demanded the federal government investigate CAIR's connection to Islamic terrorism.

"The Department of State should designate the Muslim Brotherhood and other organizations that propagate or support Islamic terrorism as terrorist organizations, and fully investigate the Council on American-Islamic Relations as an offshoot of the Muslim Brotherhood and a supporter of terrorism," Carson wrote in a policy paper in which he also called for a formal declaration of war against Islamic State.

Two months earlier Carson called for the IRS to revoke the tax-exempt status of CAIR after it demanded he withdraw as a candidate after he said a Muslim should not be elected president. "CAIR is a tax-exempt nonprofit, and the IRS rules explicitly prohibit such groups from intervening in political campaigns on behalf of – or in opposition to – a candidate," Carson said in an email to supporters.

CAIR responded by calling Carson names. "We find it interesting that Dr. Carson seeks to use a federal government agency to silence his critics and wonder if that tactic would be used to suppress First Amendment freedoms should he become president," CAIR said at the time. "CAIR is not in violation of any IRS regulation in that we did not 'participate in' or 'intervene in' any political campaign. We, as mandated by our mission as a civil rights organization, merely expressed the opinion of our community" that Carson's views made him "unfit for public office."

---

[112] "House Delegation Introduces Religious Freedom Bill," website of Rep. Don Beyer, May 11, 2016, https://beyer.house.gov/news/documentsingle.aspx?DocumentID=341, accessed May 20, 2016

[113] "House Delegation Introduces Religious Freedom Bill," website of Rep. Don Beyer, May 11, 2016, https://beyer.house.gov/news/documentsingle.aspx?DocumentID=341, accessed May 20, 2016

On Dec. 2, 2015, CAIR hastily arranged a press conference while the bodies of 14 American victims of jihad in San Bernardino, CA were still warm in order to push a media narrative that exonerated Islam in the attack.

CAIR, which the United Arab Emirates designated the year before as a terrorist group, got to work crafting a storyline about the mass-murdering Muslim married couple, Syed Rizwan Farook and Tashfeen Malik. As they fashioned a template for lazy, gullible, or sympathetic reporters to embrace, CAIR officials behaved as if Farook and Malik were strange outliers and bad Muslims.

CAIR-LA Executive Director Hussam Ayloush pretended Islam didn't inspire the attack. "We don't know the motive. Is it work, rage-related? Is it mental illness? Is it extreme ideology? At this point it's really unknown to us and it is too soon for us to speculate."

Two days later, Ayloush changed his tune, blaming America for the shootings. "Let's not forget that some of our own foreign policy, as Americans, as the West, have [sic] fueled that extremism," he told CNN's Chris Cuomo. "We are partly responsible. Terrorism is a global problem, not a Muslim problem. And the solution has to be global. Everyone has a role in it."[114]

Collaborating with Black Lives Matter

Islamic supremacists, including CAIR operatives, have been working with the violent, radical left-wing Black Lives Matter (BLM) movement since at least 2014.

The death of young Michael Brown in Ferguson, MO that summer provided Muslims an opportunity to strengthen their relationship with the movement which was created in 2012 after "white Hispanic" George Zimmerman killed black youth Trayvon Martin in self-defense in Sanford, Fla. Brown is the black, 6'4", 292-pound man who was killed by white police officer Darren Wilson on Aug. 9, 2014. When media outlets describe Brown they usually note he was unarmed and leave out the fact that he attacked Wilson and tried to seize his handgun, presumably in an effort to do the officer harm. Journalists also tend to downplay the fact that minutes before Brown assaulted Wilson, he robbed a convenience store.

The seditious collaboration in Ferguson between anti-American left-wingers, some of whom are well-funded, and anti-American Islamic supremacists, has received scant attention from the media. But Rana Baker, a writer at Electronic Intifada, explained the Marxist, identity politics-driven

---

[114] "Carson demands CAIR probe," by Matthew Vadum, FrontPageMag, Dec. 16, 2015, http://www.frontpagemag.com/fpm/261144/carson-demands-cair-probe-matthew-vadum

rationale for this cooperation between American leftists and Islamic supremacists in Ferguson. In an article filled with politically correct argot she wrote:

Unsurprisingly, many of the police deployed to crush unarmed protesters demanding justice for the brutal murder of eighteen-year-old black American Mike Brown are Israel-trained. Despotic tactics Palestinians largely associate with Israel's colonial military, such as teargassing protesters and harassing journalists, have all been implemented in Ferguson. Although Ferguson and Palestine are two different contexts, both places and their people are fighting against white supremacist regimes of oppression which continue to view them as 'disposable others' and act accordingly ... it is the moral responsibility of every Palestinian to support and foster relations with the struggles of the oppressed all over the world.[115]

Jordanian-born Palestinian Nihad Awad, co-founder and executive director of CAIR, moved to ingratiate himself with the movement by attending the funeral of Brown. Brown was not a Muslim. The Aug. 25, 2014 service that featured eulogist Al Sharpton was conducted at the Friendly Temple Missionary Baptist Church in St. Louis.

At a joint conference of the Muslim American Society (MAS) and the Islamic Circle of North America (ICNA) in December 2015, MAS executive director Khalilah Sabra urged her fellow Muslims to support BLM in order to bring about "revolution in America." Comparing the American situation to the Muslim Brotherhood-led Islamic Uprising revolutions, she said, "We are the community that staged a revolution across the world; if we can do that, why can't we have that revolution in America?" Federal prosecutors have called MAS the U.S. Muslim Brotherhood's "overt arm." ICNA also has ties to the Brotherhood and been alleged to be a front for the Pakistani Islamic political party, Jamaat-e-Islami, which was created by a leading jihadi theorist, Syed Abul A'la Maududi.[116]

The National Iranian American Council (NIAC), which is the leading U.S. defender of the jihadist Tehran regime, also hopped on the bandwagon. It brought attention to a letter that "is circulating among minority communities,

---

[115] "Intifada in Ferguson," by Matthew Vadum, FrontPageMag, Nov. 12, 2014, http://www.frontpagemag.com/fpm/245173/intifada-ferguson-matthew-vadum

[116] "Black Lives Matter and a History of Islamist Outreach to African Americans," by Kyle Shideler, Townhall, March 17, 2016, http://townhall.com/columnists/kyleshideler/2016/03/17/black-lives-matter-and-a-history-of-islamist-outreach-to-african-americans-n2135349, accessed May 29, 2016

seeking to explain why the Black Lives Matter movement is important to many first- and second-generation immigrants, many of whom are not Black themselves." The letter "seeks to show that the roots of problems affecting Black communities are the same roots of many of our own troubles." The statement continues, "NIAC believes it important to share this within our own community — as many other immigrant and minority communities are sharing with themselves — in solidarity with Black Lives Matter. As Iranian Americans face our own issues and struggle to repeal the discriminatory laws that affect us, we must also look to those who have carried the weight of minority issues in this country for centuries and do our part to help."[117]

Leftist courtesy required a smorgasbord of other activist groups to join the struggle in solidarity.

Groups endorsing Ferguson October, the 2014 festival of leftist looting and self-righteous posturing in the beleaguered St. Louis suburb, included a hodgepodge of activist organizations—many of them Saul Alinsky-inspired pressure groups—that have little or nothing to do with Ferguson, Michael Brown, or Darren Wilson. The only thing these labor movement and Occupy Wall Street activists had in common was that they were left-wing, willing to resort to violence, and seek to undermine law and order in order to bring down U.S. society.

Among them were: Action for the Common Good; Advancement Project; Alliance for a Just Society; Amnesty International; CAAAV: Organizing Asian Communities (Committee Against Anti-Asian Violence); ColorOfChange.org; Catholic Worker; Chinese Progressive Association; Coalition of Black Trade Unionists; Code Pink; Divestment Student Network; Campaign to End the Israeli Occupation; Fighting Against Natural Gas (FANG); Gamaliel Foundation; International Socialist Organization (ISO); Juvenile Urban Multicultural Program (at Syracuse University); Korean American Resource & Cultural Center; LeftRoots; Million Hoodies Movement for Justice; National Domestic Workers Alliance; National Network for Arab American Communities; National Organization for Women (NOW); New Black Panther Party; New Economy Coalition; PICO National Network; Progressive Democrats of America; Sierra Student Coalition (a project of the Sierra Club); St. Louis Palestine Solidarity Committee; Universal African Peoples Organization; United for Peace and Justice; US Action; US Palestinian Community Network; Veterans for Peace; and Working Families Party.

Many of these groups have taken money from the philanthropies of radical anti-American billionaire George Soros. Those on the rogue hedge

---

[117] "Why Black Lives Matter is important to Iranian Americans," National Iranian American Council website, July 12, 2016, http://www.niacouncil.org/black-lives-matter-important-iranian-americans/, accessed July 14, 2016

fund manager's payroll include Advancement Project, Gamaliel Foundation, NOW, and US Action.

Remnants of the ACORN activist empire, which filed for bankruptcy in 2010, were involved in organizing unrest in Ferguson. Missourians Organizing for Reform and Empowerment (MORE), a nonprofit advocacy organization, is the rebranded Missouri branch of the former Association of Community Organizations for Reform Now (ACORN) which filed for bankruptcy in 2010. That ACORN state chapter reconstituted itself in December 2009 as MORE under orders from ACORN's national headquarters. President Obama used to work for ACORN and he represented it in court as a lawyer.

MORE was in the protests and in efforts to free jailed demonstrators so they could continue vandalizing businesses, intimidating perceived adversaries, setting fires, throwing projectiles and urine at cops, and engaging in the Left's usual modes of so-called nonviolent protest. MORE believes that protesters should be given a blank check to inflict whatever harm they wish on the community in pursuit of social justice. The Working Families Party, founded in New York State in the 1990s by ACORN members, was also involved in Ferguson. It endorsed Ferguson October.[118]

Indoctrinating Children

CAIR ran into headwinds in the fall of 2015 when it demanded that public school students in overwhelmingly Christian Tennessee be taught that Islam's founder Muhammad is the one and only true messenger of God. The group claimed legislation to forbid public schools in the state from teaching the principles of Islam and every other religion until the 10th grade was bigoted and unfair to Muslims.

Aided by the Left's relentless agitation for so-called diversity and multiculturalism, the taxpayer-funded Islamization of America is well underway. CAIR isn't concerned about terrorism and theocratic totalitarianism as it lashes out at its critics, preying on Americans' sense of fair play, as well as their belief in equality and religious freedom. So naturally CAIR smeared supporters of the anti-religious indoctrination bill as bigots and Islamophobes.

The bill was introduced by Republican Sheila Butt, the Majority Floor Leader in the Tennessee House of Representatives, and author of several parenting books. Butt championed the measure after parents complained

---

[118] "Intifada in Ferguson," by Matthew Vadum, FrontPageMag, Nov. 12, 2014, http://www.frontpagemag.com/fpm/245173/intifada-ferguson-matthew-vadum

about "what they perceive as an inappropriate focus on Islam in history and social studies courses in taxpayer-funded middle schools."

"I think that probably the teaching that is going on right now in seventh, eighth grade is not age-appropriate," Butt said. Students "are not able to discern a lot of times whether it's indoctrination or whether they're learning about what a religion teaches."

Attacking Butt's proposal, CAIR government affairs manager Robert McCaw predictably sneered: "Islamophobes like Rep. Butt fail to recognize that there is a big difference between teaching students about religion as an important part of world history and promoting particular religious beliefs. The education of children in Tennessee should not be delayed because of anti-Muslim bigotry."

According to the Daily Caller, parents from across Tennessee "expressed alarm ... because their children in public middle schools are learning about the Five Pillars of Islam in a world history and social studies classes. (The first and most important pillar is the statement of faith in Islam and is roughly translated as: "There is no god but God. Muhammad is the messenger of God.") At the same time, the parents say, the course material pointedly ignores Christianity."

One of the taxpayer-supported agents of this Muslim indoctrination, Metro Nashville Public Schools social studies teacher Kyle Alexander, defended inflating the accomplishments of the Islamic world before captive, impressionable 12-year-olds. Demonstrating a superficial, politically correct understanding of Islam, he said, "[t]he reality is the Muslim world brought us algebra, 'One Thousand and One Nights,' and some can argue it helped bring about the Renaissance. There is a lot of influence that that part of the world had on world history."

While it is true that Muslim countries had an impact on world history, it isn't quite as benign as Alexander described. For example, algebra. President Obama made the same claim in his fact-averse "A New Beginning Speech" speech in 2009 in Cairo that was calculated to flatter Muslims. As Ann Coulter indignantly retorted at the time: "Operating on the liberal premise that what Arabs really respect is weakness, Obama listed Muslims' historical contributions to mankind, such as algebra (actually, that was the ancient Babylonians), the compass (that was the Chinese), pens (the Chinese again), and medical discoveries (would that be clitorectomies?)."[119]

---

[119] "CAIR demands Muslim indoctrination of 12-year-olds," by Matthew Vadum, FrontPageMag, Oct. 16, 2015, http://www.frontpagemag.com/fpm/260466/cair-demands-muslim-indoctrination-12-year-olds-matthew-vadum

CHAPTER 7

Selling the Iran Nuclear Deal through Deception

The far-left Obama administration used lies to push through a bizarre, loophole-ridden, one-sided nuclear nonproliferation pact with the Islamic Republic of Iran, long recognized as the world's leading state sponsor of terrorism. U.S. officials managed to do this even as Iranian officials openly mocked them in front of TV cameras and refused to stick to the script Obama's people gave them. All the while there were regular "death to America" and "death to Israel" rallies in Iran. Somehow the Obama administration convinced Congress and a significant chunk of the population that the theocratic totalitarian barbarians in Tehran were America's friends.

We know that underhanded, deceitful tactics were employed by the White House because President Obama's deputy national security adviser for strategic communications, Ben Rhodes, bragged about it to the *New York Times* in mid-2016.

But who is Rhodes exactly?

Rhodes long aspired to be a fiction writer. He accomplished his fabulist goal early in Obama's presidency. Rhodes wrote Obama's shamelessly ahistorical 2009 speech delivered in Cairo. "By falsifying history, he built up the Middle East and Islam, while he disparaged the United States, the West, and, of course, President George W. Bush," writes Mary Grabar. "The president who called himself a 'citizen of the world' claimed that there was no difference between the West and the Middle East, between Christianity and Islam."[120]

But greater things were to come. Rhodes came up with the "story," that is, the false narrative used to sell the Iran deal. When an Obama foreign policy initiative failed, Rhodes was called in to clean up the mess. He remained quite busy during his White House tenure.

Rhodes admitted he misled journalists about the correct timeline of U.S. negotiations in the nuclear agreement, relying upon greenhorn reporters to create an "echo chamber" in order to convince the public to support the deal. The administration put out word that moderates were suddenly in power in Iran in 2013 and that this presented a golden opportunity. It's a bald-faced lie.

Rhodes admitted the powers-that-be in Iran may not be the moderate reformers the White House claimed but bristled when the interviewer

---

[120] "How will history remember Obama's 'Cairo speech'?" by Mary Grabar, FrontPageMag, Oct. 15, 2012, http://www.frontpagemag.com/fpm/148276/how-will-history-remember-obamas-cairo-speech-mary-grabar, accessed May 1, 2016. Grabar explored the speech in depth in her 2012 book, *"A New Beginning," or a Revised Past?: Barack Obama's Cairo Speech.*

suggested he had employed deception. "Yes, I would prefer that it turns out that [President Hassan] Rouhani and [Minister of Foreign Affairs Mohammad Javad] Zarif are real reformers who are going to be steering this country into the direction that I believe it can go in, because their public is educated and, in some respects, pro-American. But we are not betting on that."

The prospect of a future administration using the same tactics frightens Rhodes. "I mean, I'd prefer a sober, reasoned public debate, after which members of Congress reflect and take a vote," he shrugged. "But that's impossible."

As the *New York Times* put it, the appearance of new moderate leadership in the former Persia "was largely manufactured for the purpose of selling the deal." The falsehood was easy to sell because reporters too often tend to be young and ignorant of the world and history and politics so they don't question what is put in front of them. "People construct their own sense of source and credibility now," said Tanya Somanader, then-Director of Digital Response in the White House Office of Digital Strategy. "They elect who [sic] they're going to believe."

In the spring of 2015 Rhodes and his colleagues came up with "legions of arms-control experts [who] began popping up at think tanks and on social media, and they became key sources for hundreds of often-clueless reporters." D.C. insiders Jeffrey Goldberg of the *Atlantic* and Laura Rozen of the pro-Iran, pro-Hizballah Al-Monitor were instrumental in promoting the false narrative. "Laura Rozen was my RSS feed," Somanader said. "She would just find everything and retweet it."

"We created an echo chamber," Rhodes said of all the instant experts. "They were saying things that validated what we had given them to say."

The dangerously anti-American Ploughshares Fund, which media outlets have been conned into labeling a "global security organization," also played a big role of in greasing the mainstream media's skids. The San Francisco-based arms control philanthropy handed out grants to several nonprofit organizations in the national security community, apparently helping to create the echo chamber to which Rhodes referred.

Who might be in that echo chamber? According to Eli Lake, lots of people. He reports that Ploughshares' messaging work on Iran got underway in 2011, long before Rhodes started reaching out to left-wing groups to shape his Iran narrative.

Beginning in August 2011, Ploughshares and its grantees formed the Iran Strategy Group. Over time this group created a sophisticated campaign to reshape the national narrative on Iran. That campaign sought to portray skeptics of diplomacy as "pro-war," and to play down the dangers of the Iranian nuclear program before formal negotiations started in 2013

only to emphasize those dangers after there was an agreement in 2015.

The strategy group, which included representatives of the Arms Control Association, the National Security Network, the National Iranian American Council, the Federation of American Scientists, the Atlantic Council and others, sought to "develop process and mechanism to implement Iran campaign strategies, tactics and narrative," according to an agenda for the first meeting of the group on Aug. 17, 2011.[121]

An Aug. 2, 2011, memo from then-National Security Network executive director Heather Hurlburt and ReThink Media co-founder Peter Ferenbach, argued that selling any U.S. deal with Iran would be "extremely difficult" because of the "media environment" on Iran. Iran got bad press in 2011, ranging from reports that it would moving forward with its nuclear program to the Department of the Treasury and a December 2011 ruling by Judge George Daniels of the Southern District of New York accusing Iran of working with al-Qa'eda, both before and after the 9/11 attacks.[122]

"We are left in the position of responding to the news headlines and parrying the negative commentary that follows," they wrote.

Lying was the best way forward, they reasoned. Smearing critics of any eventual agreement as bloodthirsty warmongers was the best approach to weaken resistance to the deal. "It would be best to describe" conservatives favoring military strikes against Iran, they wrote, as "'pro-war,' and leave it to them to back off that characterization of their position." Perhaps these message-shapers learned how to foment anti-war fever through polarization and vilification from Saul Alinsky.

"This approach became a centerpiece of the White House's own message four years later when Obama was selling his deal to Congress," Lake writes. "In a speech at American University that summer he said, 'The choice we face is ultimately between diplomacy or some form of war.'"[123]

According to philanthropy databases, Ploughshares handed out funding to the Arms Control Association ($2,215,000 since 2003, much of it earmarked for Iran-related projects), Federation of American Scientists ($1,021,000 since 2003), Atlantic Council of the United States ($625,000

[121] "The secret history of the Iran-deal 'echo chamber,'" by Eli Lake, Bloomberg, May 24, 2016, https://www.bloomberg.com/view/articles/2016-05-24/the-secret-history-of-the-iran-deal-echo-chamber, accessed June 10, 2016

[122] *Havlish vs. Osama Bin Laden, Iran, et al,* http://iran911case.com/, accessed 4 October 2016

[123] "The secret history of the Iran-deal 'echo chamber,'" by Eli Lake, Bloomberg, May 24, 2016, https://www.bloomberg.com/view/articles/2016-05-24/the-secret-history-of-the-iran-deal-echo-chamber, accessed June 10, 2016

since 2010), National Iranian American Council ($319,545 since 2007), and the National Security Network ($259,000 since 2011).

What did those Ploughshares-funded groups have to say about the agreement?

Although Ploughshares has given the Institute for Science and International Security (which has the unfortunate acronym ISIS) $698,330 since 2003, that group's president, David Albright did not give the pact a thumbs-up. Maybe Ploughshares cut him off because he wouldn't toe the line.

But other grant recipients were delighted with the agreement. In January 2016 the Arms Control Association called it "a historic milestone that strengthens the nonproliferation regime." The Atlantic Council quoted former U.S. diplomat R. Nicholas Burns as saying the pact was "a historic achievement" that "will freeze Iran's nuclear efforts." NIAC also called it "a historic achievement" and proclaimed that "for the first time in a decade, Iran's nuclear program no longer poses a threat to the United States." Ploughshares has also given National Public Radio (NPR) at least $450,000 since 2006. Two of the grants, one for $150,000 in 2011 and another for $100,000 in 2013, were earmarked for Iran-related topics. NPR claims the money in no way influenced its softball news treatment of the Iranian nuclear issue.[124]

It needs to be noted that officials at the Ploughshares Fund are longtime apologists for the world's worst dictators and are devoted to undermining U.S. national security. Ploughshares, which partners with the Institute for Policy Studies, Code Pink, J Street, and United for Peace & Justice, spent a total of $4 million in the five years before 2016 to push the pact with Iran and coordinated with the so-called peace groups and think tanks on its payroll to support the U.S.-led negotiations.

The truth is flexible to Ploughshares president Joe Cirincione. In 2007, he dismissed media reports that Syria was constructing a nuclear reactor with North Korean help, calling them propaganda spread by the U.S. and Israel. Intelligence officials later came up with video evidence proving the Syrian-North Korean collaboration.[125]

Returning to the Rhodes interview, interviewer David Samuels seemed a little uncomfortable with the Obama aide's Machiavellian swagger. Samuels wrote:

---

[124] "Ploughshares and the Iran deal echo chamber," by Lee Smith, *Weekly Standard*, May 24, 2016, http://www.weeklystandard.com/ploughshares-and-the-iran-deal-echo-chamber/article/2002528, accessed June 10, 2016

[125] "North Korea claims H-bomb success," by Matthew Vadum, FrontPageMag, Jan. 7, 2016, http://www.frontpagemag.com/fpm/261377/north-korea-claims-h-bomb-success-matthew-vadum

When I suggested that all this dark metafictional play seemed a bit removed from rational debate over America's future role in the world, Rhodes nodded. "In the absence of rational discourse, we are going to discourse the [expletive] out of this," he said. "We had test drives to know who was going to be able to carry out our message effectively, and how to use outside groups like Ploughshares, the Iran Project and whomever else. So we knew the tactics that worked." He is proud of the way he sold the Iran deal. "We drove them crazy," he said of the deal's opponents.

The ends justify the means, Rhodes believes.

The article also mentions Robert Malley, who worked closely with Rhodes on the ayatollah-empowering weapons pact. Malley is described as "a favored troubleshooter," who was the White House "point person during the later stage of the negotiations."[126]

That may be true. Malley is also a professional left-wing propagandist just like his father. Samuels puts a positive spin on this, describing the younger Malley as "a particularly keen observer of the changing art of political communication"

Malley was previously a special assistant to President Bill Clinton for Arab-Israeli affairs. He wrote a series of articles in 2001 blaming Israel – not PLO boss Yasser Arafat – for the failure of Clinton's peace efforts. Malley had previously worked for the George Soros-funded International Crisis Group and grew up in a home where Yasser Arafat, Fidel Castro, and Leonid Brezhnev were heroes and even American liberal Democrats like Jimmy Carter were villains. Malley's family had close ties to Arafat.[127]

Malley's father, Simon, who was born into a Syrian family in Cairo, was a key figure in the Egyptian Communist Party and an admirer of Arafat and Todor Zhivkov, the Soviet-era communist dictator of Bulgaria. Malley moved to Paris in 1969 and founded the Soviet-financed journal *Afrique Asie,* which supported various left-wing so-called liberation movements such as the Palestinian cause. Not surprisingly, the media outlet backed Iran's seizure of U.S. hostages, the 1979 Soviet invasion of Afghanistan, Cuban interventions

---

[126] "The aspiring novelist who became Obama's foreign-policy guru," by David Samuels, *New York Times Magazine,* May 5, 2016,

http://www.nytimes.com/2016/05/08/magazine/the-aspiring-novelist-who-became-obamas-foreign-policy-guru.html?_r=1, accessed June 5, 2016

[127] "The Robert Malley – Arafat Connection," by Alex Safian, Committee for Accuracy in Middle East Reporting in America website, Feb. 2, 2008

http://www.camera.org/index.asp?x_context=8&x_nameinnews=88&x_article=1437, accessed May 5, 2016

in Angola and Ethiopia, and the Algerian-backed guerrilla war in Morocco. *Afrique Asie* attacked Israel and the Camp David accords of 1978, moderate leaders in Africa and the Middle East, and condemned the British "aggression" against the Falkland Islands as "a classical example of colonialism." Malley wrote articles urging the assassination of heads of state and reportedly conducted a 20-hour interview with Fidel Castro.[128]

The younger Malley caused President Obama's 2008 campaign some heartburn. Brought on as a Middle Eastern policy advisor, he was promptly canned when news broke that he had been in regular communication with HAMAS. Malley may have been offered up as a scapegoat by Obama. Arabic-language newspaper *Al-Hayat* reported that Malley was secretly negotiating for months, making overtures to HAMAS on behalf of the then-Illinois senator. Malley was magically rehabilitated by 2014 when the president made him senior director of the National Security Council.[129]

Malley's history and background might be shocking but for the fact that at time of this report, President Obama had been in power for more than seven and a half years. Socialists, communists, Afro-centrists, and Islamic supremacists have been shown to have worked everywhere in the Obama administration. Another way of putting it would be to say that during that time, Malley's affiliations barely qualified as news.

People who have no business being anywhere near America's national security apparatus were embedded within it. The most dangerous radical of them all, of course, was President Obama. It now falls to the Trump administration to root out such influences within U.S. government and take U.S. policy, both foreign and domestic, in a different direction.

---

[128] "The Robert Malley – Arafat Connection," by Alex Safian, Committee for Accuracy in Middle East Reporting in America, Feb. 2, 2008

http://www.camera.org/index.asp?x_context=8&x_nameinnews=88&x_article=1437, accessed May 5, 2016; "Simon Malley" (obituary), *Guardian*, Sept. 26, 2006, https://www.theguardian.com/media/2006/sep/27/guardianobituaries.pressandpublishing, accessed Sept. 7, 2016

[129] "ISIS Czar a Terrorist Sympathizer Once Fired by Obama for Hamas Ties," Judicial Watch website, Dec. 2, 2015, https://www.judicialwatch.org/blog/2015/12/isis-czar-a-terrorist-sympathizer-once-fired-by-obama-for-hamas-ties/, accessed Sept. 7, 2016; "Adviser Fired by Obama for Hamas Meeting Gets Top WH Security Job," Judicial Watch website, Feb. 19, 2014, http://www.judicialwatch.org/blog/2014/02/adviser-fired-by-obama-for-hamas-meeting-gets-top-wh-security-job/, accessed Sept. 7, 2016

Muslims and the Left work together to do things that serve the cause of the Global Jihad Movement. This book documents how they do it. They use nonprofit groups and well-heeled foundations to weaken our will to resist.

The Left creates an alternate reality in which world temperatures claimed to be rising at an imperceptibly slow rate pose more of a threat to mankind than militants flying commercial jetliners into skyscrapers or jihadis in suits working to undermine the Constitution.

Many Americans — well, make that most Americans — have no idea how closely figures in both major political parties, government, academia, Hollywood, grassroots activism, and other fields are working, wittingly or unwittingly, to make America safe for Islam and sharia.

It's hard to blame ordinary people who aren't news or politics junkies for living in these bubbles. Even with the advent of Fox News and the alternative online media, the Left continues to maintain a death grip over the flow of information in this country. It remains culturally dominant and there is no reason to believe it will surrender its power without a fight.

With few exceptions, those in power in government are either blind to the threat that Islamic supremacism, jihad, and sharia pose to the United States and Western Civilization, indifferent to it, or willing accomplices to the Islamization process that has been moving forward in this country for years.

And that's exactly the way those planning the next 9/11 like it.

Made in the USA
Middletown, DE
04 July 2019